FAITH AND PS

For Paul and Jenny
with love

October 2005

Other titles in the series:

SERIES EDITORS: Leslie J Francis and Jeff Astley

FAITH AND PSYCHOLOGY

Personality, Religion and the Individual

Leslie J Francis

DARTON·LONGMAN+TODD

First published in 2005 by
Darton, Longman and Todd Ltd
1 Spencer Court
140–142 Wandsworth High Street
London SW18 4JJ

ISBN 0-232-52544-7

A catalogue record for this book is available from the British Library.

Designed by Sandie Boccacci
Phototypeset in Minion by Intype Libra Ltd
Printed and bound in Great Britain by
Page Bros, Norwich, Norfolk

CONTENTS

ACKNOWLEDGEMENTS

Quotations from the Bible are taken from the *New Revised Standard Version* (NRSV) Bible, copyright © 1989, by the Division of Christian Education of the National Council of the Churches of Christ in the USA, and are used by permission. All rights reserved.

The Myers-Briggs Type Indicator and MBTI are registered trademarks of Consulting Psychologists Press, Inc.

Extracts from L J Francis and P Atkins *Exploring Mark's Gospel*, Continuum, 2002, are re-printed with the publisher's permission.

PREFACE

At the beginning of the third millennium a new mood is sweeping through the Christian churches. This mood is reflected in a more radical commitment to discipleship among a laity who wish to be theologically informed and fully equipped for Christian ministry in the secular world.

Exploring Faith: theology for life is designed for people who want to take Christian theology seriously in a way that engages the mind, involves the heart, and seeks active expression in the way we live. Those who explore their faith in this way are beginning to shape a theology for life.

Exploring Faith: theology for life is rooted in the individual experience of the world and in the ways through which God is made known in the world. Such experience is related to and interpreted in the light of the Christian tradition. Each volume is written by a scholar who has clear authority in the area of theology discussed and who takes seriously the ways in which busy adults learn. The series aims to open up key aspects of theology and explore these in dialogue with the readers' own experience.

The volumes are suitable for all those who wish to learn more about the Christian faith and ministry, including those who have already taken Christian basic courses (such as *Alpha* and *Emmaus*) and have been inspired to undertake further study, those preparing to take theology as an undergraduate course, and those already engaged on degree programmes. The volumes have been developed for individuals to work on alone or for groups to study together.

Already groups of Christians are using the *Exploring Faith: theology for life* series throughout the United Kingdom, linked by exciting credit-bearing initiatives pioneered jointly by the churches and the academy. There are a number of ways in which learning Christians can find their way into award-bearing programmes through the series *Exploring Faith: theology for life.*

The series editors wish to express their personal thanks to colleagues who have helped them shape the series identity, especially Diane Drayson, Evelyn Jackson, Susan Thomas and Virginia Hearn, and to the individual authors who have produced high quality text on schedule and so generously accepted firm editorial direction. The editorial work has been supported by the North of England Institute for Christian Education and the Welsh National Centre for Religious Education.

Leslie J Francis
Jeff Astley

INTRODUCTION

In the minds of some people psychology and religion stand on opposite sides of a great valley, looking suspiciously across from one side to the other. There are good grounds for such a view. Some early psychologists took a very hostile approach to religion and some people of faith hit back with equal force. Some Christians are still engaged in that same battle.

I do not happen to share that view. I serve as an Anglican priest, committed to a view of the world shaped by faith. I am also a chartered psychologist and Fellow of the British Psychological Society, committed to professional research and practice in psychology. Such an alliance between psychology and faith is no longer unusual, as shown in the United Kingdom by the well-established Network of Christians in Psychology and by the newly formed Network for Psychological Type and Christian Faith. In the United States of America the alliance has led to the development of two first class journals, *Journal of Psychology and Christianity* and *Journal of Psychology and Theology*.

The greater danger today is no longer that of churches rejecting the insights of psychology. Instead it is the danger of churches accepting the insights of psychology too uncritically. The aim of the present book, therefore, is to provide a positive but critical introduction to the relationship between faith and psychology.

Both faith and psychology are very broad, all-embracing concepts. Putting the two concepts together creates a huge field of study. I need to be content, therefore, to illustrate such a huge field by concentrating on one aspect of it. My choice is to focus on personality psychology and on the Christian faith as expressed through churches and chapels. Personality psychology is a good choice for two reasons. First, the psychological study of personality raises key issues about what it is to be human, created in the image of God. Theology is interested in such issues as well. Second, the churches are already making good use of personality psychology in a number of creative ways. It is important to understand such developments and to evaluate them critically.

In general terms psychology is about people. In particular terms it is about *you*, the individual reader. For this reason *Faith and Psychology* invites you to embark on a disciplined journey of self-discovery as you make your way through the sequence of ten chapters. Self-discovery should lead to greater self-awareness and to increased self-acceptance. Self-discovery should lead to greater insight into others and to better acceptance of those who are so different from ourselves. Self-discovery should lead to greater theological insight into the nature of the creator God who created men and women in God's own image. In the Christian tradition, acceptance of self is neither self-indulgence nor luxury, but the starting point for fulfilling the first commandment (Mark 12:29-30). For how can we love God, if we do not love our neighbour? How can we love our neighbour if we do not first love ourselves? After all, according to Mark 12:31 Jesus said that the second commandment is this:

> You should love your neighbour as yourself.

Faith and Psychology has been structured to take the reader on a journey of exploration in four stages. The first stage of the journey begins in Chapters 1 and 2. These two chapters argue the case for theology and faith taking psychology seriously, and then introduce personality theory as a key meeting point between psychology and faith. To take psychology seriously people of faith need to be prepared to listen to how psychologists set about their work and to become familiar with the tools of the psychologist's trade.

The second stage of the journey is covered by Chapters 3 and 4. Here two quite different personality theories are introduced and their relevance and usefulness for matters of faith are explored. These two personality theories were shaped by Hans Eysenck and by Raymond Cattell.

The third stage of the journey is covered by Chapters 5, 6 and 7. Here a third theory of personality is introduced in greater depth. This is Carl Jung's theory of 'psychological type', which has become particularly well known in churches through the Myers-Briggs Type Indicator. In these chapters readers are invited to explore their own psychological type preferences. Strategically, however, psychological type is introduced only after meeting other personality theories. This sequence should help us to be more objective and openly critical about the use of psychological type theory.

The fourth stage of the journey is covered by Chapters 8, 9 and 10. Here the theory of psychological type is applied to three specific faith-related areas: the study of ministry style, the study of church congregations, and the study of Scripture and preaching.

Throughout all four stages of the journey the emphasis is on the empirical research literature and on assessing the evidence for the claims made by psychology. This whole enterprise is an exercise in *empirical theology*, written from the conviction that empirically based psychology can open up new insights into the nature, plans and purposes of God, and can help the church fulfil God's mission and ministry in the world.

I owe a great debt of gratitude to many friends and colleagues who have helped to shape and to inform my interest in psychology and faith, and in psychological type and ministry. Special gratitude is given to Tony Crockett who challenged me to think through the application of type theory for clergy development, to the three colleagues who collaborated with me on facilitating so many type workshops, Susan Jones, John Payne and Mandy Williams-Potter, and to the clergy and lay people who participated in those workshops.

I am grateful to Susan Thomas, Diane Drayson, Charlotte Craig, Mandy Robbins and Jeff Astley who have helped shape the present manuscript.

1. PSYCHOLOGY, THEOLOGY AND FAITH

Introduction

A lot of misunderstanding takes place simply because different people use the same words to mean different things. Each generation shapes words in its own way. Today when I am told that something is 'cool', I need to recognise that I am not being informed about its temperature, but about its acceptability. Likewise, each discipline shapes words in its own way. The aim of this first chapter is to become clear about how key words like 'theology', 'psychology' and 'personality' are being used.

> ### Reflecting on experience
> Picture in your mind two professors, one a professor of psychology and the other a professor of theology. What do you imagine they do? And how do you imagine they do it? What are the tools of their trade? What are the raw materials they use in their work?

All the 'ologies' are different branches of study. This part of the word comes from the Greek word *logos* meaning 'word' or 'idea'. Some of the 'ologies' are easier to get hold of than others. The professor of geology, for example, is concerned with studying the formation of the earth (from the Greek work *gē*, meaning earth). It is easy to imagine what geologists do as they pick up their sharp hammers, chisel away at the rocks, and place their specimens under the microscope. Simplistically speaking, we can recognise the subject matter of their trade (rocks) and we can recognise the tools they use (hammers and chisels).

What is theology?

The professor of theology is altogether a more problematic creature. Literally speaking, the job of the theologian is to study God, since the word theology is based on the Greek word *theos*, meaning God. Just as the geologist studies rocks, so, it may be thought, the theologian studies God. The problem is clearly that God cannot be approached in the same way as rocks. Hammers and chisels may be of little practical value in the hands of theologians.

Because God eludes direct study, in the fashion that rocks can be studied, theologians need to look for different forms of the subject matter of their trade. Instead of putting God directly under the microscope (so to speak), theologians put the religious experience of God's people under the microscope. Different branches of theology then begin to shape different tools to examine different aspects of the way in which God is thought to be revealed and made known in the world. In the Christian tradition God is thought to be made known especially through the Scriptures of the Old Testament and the New Testament and through the traditions of the Church.

Some theologians will, therefore, spend their time absorbed, for example, in the study of the Bible, or perhaps more narrowly in the study of the New Testament, or perhaps more narrowly still in the study of John's gospel. Other theologians will spend their time absorbed in the study of Church History, or perhaps more narrowly in the study of the Patristic Period, or perhaps more narrowly still in the study of St Augustine. All in their own ways make significant contributions to how we understand God's activity in the world and God's revelation to the people of God.

A crucial distinction, however, needs to be made between the professor of theology and the minister of religion. Sometimes the same individual carries both roles, but this need not be the case and often is not the case. The professor of theology is not generally these days required to believe or practise faith. The minister of religion is not always expected to do good academic theology. The point is simply that different criteria apply in the academy and in the church. When in the lecture room, the job of the professor of theology is to test the claims made by faith and to do so with intellectual honesty and rigour. When in the pulpit the job of the minister of religion is to apply the insights of theological scholarship to nurturing the religious formation of God's people.

What is psychology?

The professor of psychology may have much more in common with the professor of theology than with the professor of geology. If the professor of geology studies solid objects like rocks and the professor of theology studies the altogether more elusive subject matter of God, what is it that the professor of psychology studies? The clue is once again given in the root of the word, this time the Greek word *psyche*, meaning soul or mind. Literally speaking, the job of the psychologist is to study the human mind.

EXERCISE
Now return to your picture of the professor of psychology and develop further your ideas of what psychologists do, and how they do it. How can they study the human mind, and what tools would be appropriate?

Like God, the human mind can be highly elusive. We cannot point to a human mind (as an example of what psychologists study) in the same direct way that we can point to a rock (as an example of what geologists study). Just as the theologian has to point not directly to God, but to the evidence of God's involvement in the world, so the psychologist has to point not directly to the human mind, but to the evidence of that mind's existence in more easily recognised behaviours.

Instead of putting the human mind directly under the microscope (so to speak), psychologists put different pieces of evidence under the microscope, all of which may reveal something of significance about the nature and functioning of the human mind. Different branches of psychology then begin to shape different tools to examine different aspects of the evidence. One branch of psychology may be concerned with the chemistry of the human brain, another branch of psychology may be interested in the processes of intellectual thought, and yet another branch of psychology may be interested in the development of human feelings and emotion. All in their own ways make significant contributions to how we understand what it is to be human.

Two crucial distinctions, however, need to be made between different ways in which the term 'psychologist' is used loosely today. The first distinction is between normal psychology and abnormal psychology.

Normal psychology is concerned with the functioning of normal healthy individuals. Abnormal psychology is concerned with the treatment of abnormal sick individuals. Normal psychology is concerned with mental health. Abnormal psychology is concerned with mental illness. It is a serious mistake to believe that all psychologists are concerned with mental illness or with pathology. Clinical psychologists have a proper role in the health service alongside other clinical professions. Industrial psychologists may be concerned with improving the performance and health of the workforce. Educational psychologists may be concerned with the development of better teaching and learning techniques.

The second distinction is between the professor of psychology and the practising psychologist. This distinction is not dissimilar from the distinction between the professor of theology and the minister of religion. When in the academy the psychologist is required to test the claims of psychology with full intellectual rigour and honesty. When in the hospital, factory or school, the job of the psychologist is to apply the insights of psychological research to promoting psychological health and to combating mental illness.

EXERCISE
Think about these definitions of psychology and of theology. Then draw up a list of ways in which the two disciplines might come into conflict with each other. Draw up a second list of ways in which theology and the church might benefit from psychology.

Psychology's response to religion

Given these working definitions of psychology and theology, how can psychology respond to religion? Is psychology necessarily hostile to religion? Or is psychology necessarily sympathetic to religion? There are three important observations in response to these questions.

First, it is important to be clear about the proper boundaries which need to be drawn around the disciplines. One of the key jobs of the theologian is to test the truth claims that are made about the nature of God. One of the key jobs of the psychologist is to test the truth claims that are made about the nature and functioning of the human mind. The psychologist is no more professionally equipped than the geologist to make pronouncements about the truth of religious claims. Of course, as normal human beings, psychologists will have their own opinions on the value of religion, but it is important to remember that working as professional people, sticking to their own trade, psychologists have nothing to say about the truth of religious claims. In this sense, properly conducted, psychology is neutral to religious faith.

Second, there are very clear points at which religions may make claims about the subject matter with which psychologists are concerned. In other words, religion may make claims which psychologists can and should assess. Suppose, for example, religion were to make claims to offer people real support in times of bereavement. Here is an *empirical question*, which psychologists can examine. Does religion actually deliver support in times of bereavement or does it not? What is being tested here, however, is a clear claim about the practical benefit of religion, and nothing more. Whatever empirical evidence is found for or against this claim, such evidence cannot be extrapolated to demonstrate the truth or falsity of the existence of God.

Third, there are also very clear examples when the beliefs and practices of religious traditions may have obvious implications for the subject matter with which psychologists are concerned. In other words, religion may have an impact, positively or negatively, on human functioning which psychologists can and should assess. Suppose, for example, a religious group were to advocate long periods of extreme fasting. Psychologists may have a responsibility to monitor the nature of the altered states of consciousness engendered and to draw attention to the points at which such religious practice could become unhealthy for the individuals or for wider society.

Theology's response to psychology

Once again, given our working definitions of psychology and theology, how can theology respond to psychology? Is psychology completely irrelevant to the concerns of the theologian? Or are there proper and valuable points of contact between the two disciplines? Again there are three important observations in response to these questions.

First, theology is able to learn from psychology in order to evaluate some of the claims made about the impact of faith on people's lives. Some of my own psychological research and that of my colleagues has been consistently picked up by the media in recent years precisely because the research has provided concrete evidence regarding the value of religion in people's lives. One strand of this research shows that religious people are generally happier than people who are not religious (Francis, Jones and Wilcox, 2000). Another strand of this research shows that young people who pray also benefit from a greater sense of purpose in life (Francis, 2004a). Purpose in life is important because young people who have a sense of purpose in life develop more pro-social values and display less anti-social behaviour.

Second, theology is able to draw on insights from psychology to shape many areas of ministry and mission. For example, psychological approaches to faith development can help the process of Christian learning (see Astley and Francis, 1992). Psychological approaches to Christian ministry can help to support clergy health and effectiveness (see Francis and Jones, 1996). Psychological approaches to the study of the Bible and preaching can help in the communication of the Gospel (see Francis, 2003).

Third, and most interestingly, psychological research can itself become a key tool for theological enquiry. If theologians take serious-ly the doctrine of creation, which claims that men and women are created in God's image, then serious psychological research into the creature may help to provide proper theological data about the nature of the creator. This is the case argued by some proponents of 'empirical theology' (see Francis, 2002).

Personality psychology

In order to explore the relationship between psychology and faith in greater depth, this book proposes to concentrate on one major branch of psychology, personality psychology. In order to understand what personality psychology is all about, we need once again to start with the question of definitions.

EXERCISE
Brainstorm the kind of words you would use to describe some-one's personality. Try creating two lists, a list of positive descriptors and a list of negative descriptors.

In everyday speech, people tend to use the word 'personality' very broadly and very generally. Personality psychology has tended to develop the word in a much narrower and more focused way. One helpful way through the debate is to distinguish between two different concepts, the concept of personality and the concept of character.

In psychology, personality tends to refer to deep-seated underlying human characteristics. *Personality* lies at the heart of who we are, or (as theologians might want to say) at the heart of how we are made. Personality describes basic individual differences, at a level of being over which we may have very little personal control. In this sense, individual differences in personality are value neutral. Take one well-established descriptor of personality, the distinction between introversion and extraversion. Personality theory does not say that extraverts are (in any sense) better or worse than introverts. Introverts and extraverts are just different and, as a consequence, introverts can do some things better than extraverts and extraverts can do some things better than introverts. In other words, introverts do not need to become extraverts in order to be better people, nor do extraverts need to become introverts in order to be better people.

Character, however, can be understood in quite a different way. While personality is value neutral, character is heavily value laden. An extravert can develop a good character (showing qualities like love, joy, peace, patience, kindness, generosity, faithfulness, gentleness and self-control), or an extravert can develop a bad character (showing qualities like licentiousness, strife, jealousy, anger, quarrels, envy and drunkenness). An introvert has equal opportunities to develop a good character (sharing the fruits of the Spirit) or to develop a bad character (sharing the works of the flesh), as described in Galatians 5:19-23.

Determinism or transformation

One of the objections that Christians sometimes raise against the use of personality psychology in the churches is that personality theory appears to be 'deterministic'. In other words, personality theory may claim to describe individuals as they are and suggest that they are not open to change. The Gospel, they argue, is all about the invitation to repentance, the possibility for change and the hope for transformation.

This objection is based on a fundamental confusion between personality and character. Clearly the Gospel really is about repentance, change and transformation as far as character is concerned. But at the same time the Gospel is about the acceptance of self as created in the image of God.

Another way to think about individual differences in personality is to conceptualise these on a par with other basic individual differences like sex and race.

EXERCISE
📖 **Read Genesis 1:27.**

So God created humankind in his image,
in the image of God he created them;
male and female he created them.
How would a theology of creation built on this text understand the individual difference known as sex?

The Church has for centuries struggled with evaluating the fundamental individual difference known as sex. The matter has not been helped by the two very different accounts of creation in the book of Genesis. One account (Genesis 2) thinks of Adam being created first and Eve being derived from Adam. The other account (Genesis 1) thinks of men and women both being created in the image of God. Today's Church, however, tends to accept and promote the equal status of men and women in the eyes of God (until, of course, it comes to the question of ordination to priesthood or to episcopacy).

The Church has for centuries struggled with evaluating the fundamental individual difference known as race. The matter has not been helped by specific traditions in the Old Testament which have promoted the subjugation of Gentile tribes and even the total obliteration of Israel's enemies. Today's Church, however, tends to accept and promote the equal status of different races in the eyes of God. Certainly there is little tendency to demand that individuals should repent and change their race.

Once personality has been conceptualised as a basic individual difference on a par with sex and race, and also clearly distinguished from character, it may become less problematic for Christians to welcome the insights which personality psychology can offer into the rich diversity of God's creation and into God the creator.

Personality and character

Another way of exploring the distinction between personality and character, in both a psychological and a theological sense, is to turn to the gospels and to re-visit Jesus' profound insight into individual differences. This insight comes through perhaps most obviously in Luke's gospel, but it is clearly there in the other gospels as well.

EXERCISE
📖 Read Luke 18:9-14, 10:38-42 and 15:11-32.

Here are three examples of Jesus' insight into human individual differences. What can you detect about the interaction between personality and character in these well-drawn narratives?

In the passage from Luke 18, Jesus contrasts some basic individual differences observable in two visitors to the temple.

> Two men went up to the temple to pray, one a Pharisee and the other a tax collector. The Pharisee, standing by himself was praying thus, 'God, I thank you that I am not like other people, thieves, rogues, adulterers . . .' But the tax collector, standing far off, would not even look up to heaven.

Jesus' interest in this narrative is one based almost entirely on character, rather than on personality. The personality psychologist might well search for clues about the personality profile of the two men, but insufficient data are provided by Luke to enable much progress to be made. We could argue that an extravert might feel more comfortable standing up and praying out loud (the Pharisee), while an introvert might feel more comfortable standing far off (the tax collector), but this would be to miss the point of the story entirely. Jesus is not concerned so much with how these two characters say what they say, but with what they say. It is their words which give insight into their character.

The moral theologian, however, will find in this passage key insights about the attitude of mind and about the stuff of character, which display being in the right relationship with God. Jesus concludes this teaching with the telling evaluation that it was the tax collector who returned to his home justified (in the right relationship with God) rather than the Pharisee.

> For all who exalt themselves will be humbled, but all who humble themselves will be exalted.

In the passage from Luke 10, Jesus contrasts some basic individual differences observable in two sisters. Jesus entered a certain village where:

> Martha welcomed him into her home. She had a sister named Mary, who sat at the Lord's feet and listened to what he was saying. But Martha was distracted by her many tasks; so she came to him and asked, 'Lord, do you not care that my sister has left me to do all the work by myself? Tell her then to help me.'

Jesus' interest in this narrative could be based on personality as well as character. Martha is portrayed as the extraverted sister. She is the one who welcomes visitors into the home. She is the one who is concerned with getting the social context right, having a feast and having contented guests. Mary is portrayed as the introverted sister. She is the one who feels at home sitting and listening, while others do the talking.

Clearly both sisters have important gifts to offer to Jesus out of the richness of their individual differences in personality. Jesus needs and welcomes the activity of the extravert. Jesus needs and welcomes the attention of the introvert.

Both sisters, however, can be equally accused of showing flaws in their character. Mary becomes so wrapped up in her own introversion that she fails to notice and to respond to the growing tension in her sister. Martha becomes so wrapped up in her own extraversion that she fails to respect and to allow space for her sister's thirst for solitude and peace with Jesus. Just by the very nature of their differing personalities, introverts and extraverts often find it difficult to appreciate how things really look, how things really feel, from the other perspective or from the other's point of view.

Both sisters show flaws in their character because of their failure to recognise and to respect individual differences. The extravert Martha just cannot understand why Mary does not see things her way and do things her way. The introvert Mary just cannot understand why Martha does not see things her way and do things her way. Personality psychology is needed to remind Martha that introverts are not failed extraverts, and to remind Mary that extraverts are not failed introverts.

In Luke 10 the conflict between extravert Martha and introvert Mary comes to a head when the extravert Martha speaks out her frustration and invites Jesus to take sides in the eternal battle between extraversion and introversion.

> Lord, do you not care that my sister has left me to do all the work by myself? Tell her then to help me.

Martha's outburst could be paraphrased thus:

> Lord, do you not care that my sister sees things in a different way from me, and prefers to live life in a different way from me? Tell her it is wrong to be an introvert and that she needs to be more like me.

Jesus' response to Martha has been the subject of much debate among the commentators, and matters are not helped by some important disagreements among different ancient manuscripts regarding Jesus' actual words. Some commentators have seen Jesus' response as placing a higher value on the contemplative tradition (represented by Mary) than on the more active tradition (represented by Martha), but this is not the only interpretation. What is clear, however, is that Jesus refused to side with Martha and to tell Mary that she needed to change her personality.

In the passage from Luke 15 Jesus contrasts some basic individual differences observable in two brothers. Jesus said:

> There was a man who had two sons. The younger of them said to his father, 'Father, give me the share of the property that will belong to me.' So he divided his property between them.

Jesus' interest in this narrative could also be based on personality, as well as character. The way in which we read this narrative today, however, is likely to be highly coloured by the context in which we first encountered it. To some people this narrative is known as the 'Parable of the Prodigal Son'. The very title focuses attention on the character flaws in the younger son. Here is the 'young waster', who needs to be taught a lesson or two in the school of life. Here is the 'young waster' who needs to repent and to re-shape his character.

To some people the narrative is known as the 'Parable of the Lost Son'. In Luke's compilation of material, the narrative stands in the third of a sequence, following the lost sheep and the lost coin. Now the very title refocuses attention on the concern of God to seek what is lost and to bring others into the kingdom.

The narrative might, however, be better styled as the 'Parable of the

T wo Sons'. In this narrative Luke includes a great deal of detail about the personalities of the two sons, and on close examination they emerge as different as chalk and cheese. In fact their personality profiles are the very mirror image, one of the other. For example, the younger son, who ventures out to strange places and to meet strange people, displays all the outgoing characteristics of the extravert. The older son, on the other hand, who is content to stay in the relative iso-lation and solitude of the home farm, displays all the inward-looking characteristics of the introvert.

If this analysis holds good regarding the basic individual differences in the personality profiles of the two sons, two other aspects of the nar-rative become of central importance. The first observation is that both sons, not just the younger son, revealed fundamental flaws in their characters. Both were profoundly uncaring toward the father: the younger son when he left home and the older son when he refused to join the celebration. Both needed to hear the call to repentance and to change their character. The second observation is that the father loved and accepted both sons in spite of their flawed characters and in light of their individual differences in personality.

Conclusion

This chapter has examined the different activities in which theologians and psychologists engage and has argued that there are good grounds for sympathy and collaboration between the two disciplines. This chapter has then argued that the study of personality provides a good example of how psychology and faith can interact. The aim of the next chapter is to examine how personality psychologists set about their business.

Further reading

Argyle, M (2000), *Psychology and Religion: an introduction*, London, Routledge.

Beit-Hallahmi, B and Argyle, M (1997), *The Psychology of Religious Belief and Experience*, London, Routledge.

Brown, L B (1988), *The Psychology of Religion: an introduction*, London, SPCK.

Francis, L J and Astley, J (eds) (2001), *Psychological Perspectives on Prayer: a read-er*, Leominster, Gracewing.

Francis, L J and Jones, S H (eds) (1996), *Psychological Perspectives on Christian Ministry: a reader*, Leominster, Gracewing.

Loewenthal, K M (2002), *The Psychology of Religion: a short introduction*, Oxford, One World.

Paloutzian, R E (1996), *Invitation to the Psychology of Religion* (second edition), Needham Heights, Massachusetts, Allyn and Bacon.

Watts, F, Nye, R and Savage, S (2002), *Psychology for Christian Ministry*, London, Routledge.

Wiles, M (1976), *What is Theology?*, Oxford, Oxford University Press.

Wulff, D M (1997), *Psychology of Religion: classic and contemporary views* (second edition), New York, John Wiley and Sons.

2. PSYCHOLOGY, PERSONALITY AND THE INDIVIDUAL

Introduction

Having decided to focus on the broad field of personality psychology, we need to make two further choices. First, there are two broad traditions within which personality can be discussed. One broad tradition is grounded in clinical experience and can be traced back through pioneers like Freud. The other broad tradition is grounded in the scientific observation of large groups of people and can be traced through pioneers like Raymond Cattell in the United States of America and Hans Eysenck in the United Kingdom. The first broad tradition reflects a concern with abnormal psychology and mental illness. The second broad tradition reflects a concern with normal psychology and psychological well-being.

The present book plans to concentrate on the second of these two traditions. It provides an introduction to the kind of personality psychology which assesses personality by means of carefully constructed personality tests and which can employ those tests (and the theories on which they build) in a range of practical situations. Chapters 5 onwards will focus specifically on the theory of 'psychological type', as assessed, for example, by the Myers-Briggs Type Indicator and by other similar measures of psychological type.

Before turning to the specific personality theory of psychological type, however, the aim of this second chapter is to enable the ideas of psychological type to be set alongside the broader family of personality theories to which it most closely relates. In this way the strengths and weaknesses of psychological type theory can be more fairly assessed. This means not only examining other personality theories, but also examining the grounds on which those theories are built. How do we assess whether or not they are true? This means raising some issues about the scientific approach to psychology and about the use of statistics and research methods.

Reflecting on experience

Chapter 1 has already referred on a number of occasions to the individual difference characterised as introversion and extraversion. What do you understand by this difference and how helpful do you find these concepts in understanding yourself and in understanding other people?

Why introversion and extraversion?

The distinction between introversion and extraversion is a useful way in which to introduce the discussion of personality psychology for two reasons. First, although among different schools of personality psychology there tends to be considerable disagreement about the number of personality factors worth discussing (or the labels by which these factors are best known), there is general agreement that extraversion and introversion should be numbered and named among them. Extraversion appears in the models of personality proposed by Hans Eysenck (see Eysenck and Eysenck, 1985), by Raymond Cattell (see Cattell, Eber and Tatsuoka, 1970) and by Costa and McCrae (1985), as well as in the instruments in the tradition of psychological type theory (see Myers and McCaulley, 1985).

Second, extraversion and introversion make a good place to begin because these technical terms have slipped into everyday usage and many people now share a common-sense understanding of what they mean. Yet caution is needed, since once again it is all too easy for people to be misled when they are using the same word, but meaning somewhat different things by it. In the technical vocabulary of personality psychologists, even the words 'introversion' and 'extraversion' can take on highly specialised overtones. We shall discover shortly that the Eysenck Personality Questionnaire and the Myers-Briggs Type Indicator use these two well-established terms in highly distinctive ways.

Although introversion and extraversion have a secure place in the different models of personality proposed by Eysenck, by Cattell, by Costa and McCrae, and by the theory of psychological type, in other ways these models differ greatly one from another, both in the number of personality variables they choose to describe and in the nature of these variables. In his pioneering work, Raymond Cattell chose to describe a total of 16 primary order personality factors, which in turn led to four higher order factors (of which extraversion was one). Beginning from a very different set of assumptions, Hans Eysenck began his pioneering work by arguing that individual differences in personality could be most adequately and economically summarised in terms of two higher order factors (of which extraversion was one). Subsequently Eysenck expanded his model to three higher order factors (keeping the place of extraversion). More recently, the Big Five model of personality proposed by Costa and McCrae (1988) has concentrated on five factors (of which extraversion is one). The model of personality provided by the theory of psychological type concentrates on four personality variables (of which extraversion-introversion is one).

Psychology as a science

There is a sense in which everyone who is discussing the human mind is engaging in psychology. We may all have opinions about the human mind, and about the structure of personality. What, however sets apart the views and the models of personality shaped by Hans Eysenck, Raymond Cattell, Costa and McCrae, or Myers and McCaulley? The answer comes in terms of the scientific nature of their enquiry and their use of publicly accepted tools to establish and to test scientific truth.

EXERCISE

Examine the above claim that psychology is a science. What makes psychology a science?

How do scientists set about establishing and testing what is true and what is false?

The scientific study of human personality begins with the natural approaches of observation and classification. But then the quest for scientific objectivity pushes further to go beyond classification to measurement, and measurement makes available to the personality psychologist all the sophisticated techniques of mathematical analysis. It was building on these techniques, which were so crucial in establishing the physical sciences, that pushed forward discovery and development in the social sciences.

The differing models of personality shaped by Hans Eysenck, Raymond Cattell, Costa and McCrae, and Myers and McCaulley are all based on the development of measuring tools. They all argue, for example, that in one way or another it is possible to measure individual differences in extraversion or introversion.

What these theories also share in common is the view that personality refers to deep-seated and covert underlying predispositions which help to shape human behaviour and, in part, help to account for the relative stability and predictability of a range of individual differences. The construct of introversion-extraversion, for example, does not apply to a simple entity which can itself be observed. It is the behaviour patterns to which this construct gives rise that can be observed.

The key notion behind personality theory is that it is possible to identify the behaviours which most consistently illustrate the various underlying personality constructs. A personality test which sets out to measure introversion-extraversion would, therefore, identify a range of sharply focused questions which tease out most effectively the introverts from the extraverts. A good question to signal introversion might be something like this: 'Are you mostly quiet when with other people?' A good question to signal extraversion might be something like this: 'Do you enjoy going out a lot?'

EXERCISE
Draw up a set of questions which illustrate your current understanding of extraversion and introversion. Consider how your friends might choose to answer these questions. How would you choose to answer them?

Brainstorming a set of questions is a good way to start off a new psychological test, but there is a long way to go after that. Eysenck's experimental way of working, for example, would now require collecting responses to these questions from a wide range of people and subjecting their responses to statistical analyses. Two statistical tools are of particular importance in this process: factor analysis and item analysis.

Factor analysis is used to check how many distinct factors the items in the test produce. One of the technical debates about extraversion, for example, concerns whether what Eysenck styles extraversion should be seen as one pure factor, or whether it should be broken down into the two component parts of sociability and impulsivity. Factor analysis can help to sort out these kinds of questions.

Item analysis helps to check that each item is really pulling its weight in the test. For example, some items may fail to measure the construct well because too few people agree with them or too few people disagree with them. Some items may be more peripheral to the construct being assessed and, therefore, fail to perform in a consistent and predictable way alongside the other items. In refining a test, a psychologist will drop items that perform poorly and try to devise items that perform better. Developing a psychological test is a complex matter.

Reliability and validity

The two technical criteria which a psychological test needs to pass are those of reliability and validity. The family of personality tests developed by Hans Eysenck, Raymond Cattell, Costa and McCrae, and Myers and McCaulley are generally considered to pass these tests, although the academic debate continues to rage as to just how well they have passed.

The idea of *reliability* concerns just how much the test can be relied on to produce the same results on different occasions. A good example of a reliable measure is the metre ruler. A lamppost that measures exactly six metres today is likely to measure exactly six metres tomorrow. Neither the metric of the ruler nor the height of the lamppost is likely to change. Another good example of a reliable measure is the mercury thermometer. Placed in boiling water at sea level today the thermometer is likely to record one hundred degrees centigrade. Tomorrow it is likely to record the same measurement. Psychological tests are never as accurate as that for two reasons. The ideas which psychological tests are attempting to measure are less tangible than the ideas represented by height or by temperature. It is likely that psychological ideas like personality are themselves less stable than physical ideas like height.

In response to this problem, psychologists have tried to devise measures of reliability against which individual tests can be assessed. The original measure was known as *test-retest reliability*. In other words, the same test was administered on two separate occasions to the same individuals and the two scores obtained for each individual were correlated. A high correlation indicates good reliability and a low correlation indicates poor reliability.

There are, however, two main problems with the test-retest model of testing reliability. On the one hand, if the two test administrations are close together, respondents may on the second occasion remember the test and their responses from the first occasion and simply repeat their earlier answers. On the other hand, if the two test administrations are separated by a longer time, then all sorts of experiences may have actually changed the ways in which some individuals feel about themselves and consequently how they respond to some of the questions in the test.

The most general response to these problems today is to prefer to examine test reliability by examining the internal performance of the items and by assessing internal consistency reliability. The statistic generally quoted is the 'alpha coefficient', originally proposed by Cronbach (1951). Perfect reliability would be represented by an alpha coefficient of 1.0, but this is never achieved in practice. Different commentators tend to accept as reliable those tests which routinely achieve an alpha coefficient of 0.7 (Kline, 1993) or 0.65 (de Vellis, 2003).

The idea of *validity* concerns just how much a test really measures what it claims to measure. A reliable test is not necessarily a valid one, but an unreliable test can never claim to provide a valid measurement.

The idea of establishing the validity of a personality test is highly complex. We can test the validity of the thermometer against boiling water because we can see the water boil, but how can a measure of something as elusive as introversion or extraversion be validated?

EXERCISE

Think about the problem of how to assess the validity of a psychological test which claims to measure extraversion and introversion. How would you go about such a task?

There are two main approaches to trying to establish the validity of psychological tests. The first approach is known as *criterion validity*. The criterion is the external feature against which the test is assessed. In this sense, the thermometer is validated against the criterion measure of the boiling water. But what criterion measure can serve to validate a test designed to assess extraversion and introversion? One answer to this question is to gather a group of known extraverts and a group of known introverts. It should be the case that the group of known extraverts will record high scores on the test of extraversion, while the group of known introverts will record low scores on the same test.

This kind of criterion validation of the measure of extraversion is not quite as simple and self-evident as it may first appear. How do we define the two groups of extraverts and introverts in the first place? How sure can we be that these two groups of people have enough self-insight to stand up to the responsibility of measuring the test against them? Suppose introversion and extraversion were more like blood pressure, where the scientific assessment of blood pressure is more accurate than self-assessment. Then discrepancies between the scores of extraversion and the criterion groups might as likely cast doubt on the validity of the criterion groups as on the validity of the test.

The second approach is known as *construct validity*. This method of establishing the validity of a test is more complex and more time consuming, but also more secure. Construct validity begins by unpacking the nature of the construct (or idea) being assessed, say in this case extraversion. What is extraversion? How would we expect extraverts to behave? Unpacking the construct leads to the development of a series of hypotheses about how extraversion functions in relationship to other constructs. Then it is possible to set about testing this series of hypotheses.

Suppose, for example, that our understanding of introversion and extraversion implies that introverts are likely to enjoy studying alone and prefer to learn by reading books rather than by talking things over in the pub. We might decide to test this hypothesis by inviting students to report on their reading habits and on the frequency with which they go to the pub. Of course, the relationship between extraversion and reading, or between extraversion and going to the pub, will not be a straightforward matter. There will be many other 'contaminating' variables that get in the way. Nonetheless, we are likely to find a small but statistically significant correlation coefficient between the extraversion scores and these other factors. This provides some supporting evidence for the construct validity of our measure.

Using statistics

By this stage it has become abundantly clear that a proper appreciation and evaluation of personality theories requires at least an elementary knowledge of statistics. Already we have referred to factor analysis, to item analysis, to correlation coefficients and to alpha coefficients. There are a number of other technical statistical terms often used in the literature which need to be grasped before going further into the use of personality psychology. Readers who already know about such things may choose to skip the next few pages, but those who do not know about them should pause for a while just to make sure.

EXERCISE

Make a list of the statistical or mathematical terms with which you are familiar and then prepare a short definition of these terms. Start with terms like multiply, divide, average and percentage.

Levels of measurement

Statisticians recognise that numbers can be used in a variety of different ways, and distinguish between at least four different levels of measurement, known as nominal, ordinal, interval and ratio. The *nominal* use of numbers occurs when, for example, runners wear numbered shirts. The numbers are used quite randomly as 'names' to distinguish one runner from another. There is no sense of progression in which these numbers are used. The *ordinal* use of numbers is when there is a sense of progression, but no grounds to assume that the space between each number is equal. For example, the person who comes first in a test may get a mark of 84%, the person who comes second may get a mark of 76% and the person who comes third may get a mark of 75%. Clearly these three candidates are ranked in order, but the distances between them are not the same. The *interval* use of numbers is when it can be assumed that the space between each number is equal. This happens, for example, on the ruler. The space between six and seven is the same as between three and four, just one centimetre in each case. Finally, the ratio use of numbers is when there is a fixed zero. Generally scores recorded on a personality scale are assumed to approximate the interval level of measurement. But it remains a matter of contention as to whether the space between extraversion scores of ten and eleven is really the same as the space between extraversion scores of three and four.

One further observation needs to be made about the level of measurement achieved by personality measures. The scores are always anchored to and limited by the instrument which generated them. For example, Eysenck has developed a series of extraversion scales, having different numbers of items. An extraversion score of six recorded on a twelve-item extraversion scale cannot meaningfully be compared with a score of six recorded on a longer 24-item extraversion scale.

Similarly, it is not sensible to compare scores recorded on different scales generated by the same personality test. For example, the Eysenck Personality Questionnaire will produce scores of extraversion, neuroticism and psychoticism. An individual who scores six on extraversion, eight on neuroticism and three on psychoticism cannot be said to be more neurotic than psychotic. These individual scores can only be interpreted against the population norms, that is to say against information published in the test manual about how people in general score on the test.

Central tendency and dispersion

The average value of a set of numbers is known as the *mean*. It is calculated by adding together all the numbers and then dividing by the number of observations. Take the following set of numbers: 1, 8, 12, 19, 44, 44, 45 and 51. There are 8 numbers in this set and they add up to 224. The mean is therefore 224 divided by 8, or 28.

The number which occurs most often is known as the *mode*. In the above example it is 44. The number which divides the data set in half, so that 50% of the observations lie to one side of this point and 50% lie to the other side, is called the *median*. In the above example it is half way between 19 and 44, namely 31.5.

The mean is the most often quoted measure of central tendency, but the mean alone is not a sufficient summary of a set of numbers. Take the following set of numbers: 1, 2, 4, 7, 18, 18, 28, 150. Like the first set the mean is 28, but the dispersion is quite different. The *standard deviation* gives an estimate of the average distance of the numbers from the mean. The larger the standard deviation, the greater the spread of numbers.

Probability

The idea of probability helps us to check whether the findings from statistical studies can be trusted, or whether they are likely to have arisen by chance.

EXERCISE

Take a coin and toss it ten times. How many heads, how many tails? You may have found by chance that you had three heads and seven tails. Could you conclude from these data that your coin has twice as many tails as heads? Now toss the coin 100 times and you are quite likely to find that you have 50 heads and 50 tails, or 49 and 51.

If you administer a personality test to 20 clergy and to 20 students and find that the mean score for clergy is ten, but for the students it is twelve, can you conclude that clergy are less extraverted than students? You need some method of testing whether this difference, given the number of subjects and given the means and standard deviations of these scores, could have occurred by chance. There are different kinds of statistical tests for checking different kinds of questions, but they all need to be related to estimates of probability.

Good scientific studies in personality psychology will, therefore, routinely offer probability levels with their findings. The minimum level of probability generally accepted is the 5% level, expressed as $P<.05$. This means that the statistical finding could occur by chance five times in a hundred. Other standard levels reported in the literature are the 1% level ($P<.01$) and the 0.1% level ($P<.001$). These mean respectively that the findings could have occurred by chance once in a hundred times and once in a thousand times. In other words, probability levels provide a measure of how unlikely it is for the findings to have occurred by chance.

Statistical tests

The statistical tests most frequently used in personality studies include the t-test, the correlation coefficient, and the chi square coefficient.

The *t-test* (t) is used to examine the way in which two sets of means differ, say the extraversion scores of clergymen and the extraversion scores of students. It takes into account the number of observations, the means and the standard deviations. The t-test is then used to establish the probability level.

The *correlation coefficient* (r) is used to examine the way in which two sets of scores on different scales co-vary, say the way in which extraversion scores co-vary with scores of enjoying long periods of silent meditation. Two kinds of information are provided by the correlation coefficient, concerning the strength of the relationship and the likelihood of the relationship occurring by chance. First, the perfect relationship is represented by 1.0 and a complete lack of relationship by 0.0. There may be a positive relationship between extraversion and liking church social events, represented, say, by a correlation of +0.32. There may be a negative relationship between extraversion and liking long periods of silent meditation, represented, say, by a correlation of −0.26. Second, the correlation coefficient is used to establish the probability level.

The *chi square test* (χ^2) is used to examine the relationship between two nominal variables, say sex and denomination. Is there a significant difference, for example, between the number of men who describe themselves as Baptist or as Elim, compared with the number of women? Once again, the chi square test is used to establish the probability level.

Research design

One further set of issues needs to be raised before we are in a strong position to evaluate how good the research really is that underpins our understanding of personality theory and the application of that theory to matters of faith. These are issues concerned with research design. They include matters like sampling, response rate, the appropriateness of claims made on the basis of individual studies, ethical concerns, and the role of replication studies.

EXERCISE

Why do you imagine that the response rate to a survey is so important to report? What would you consider to be a realistic response rate to aim for, and what are your reasons for this view?

Population and sample

The population refers to a complete set of people and needs to be defined very carefully. We could imagine research being concerned with establishing just how extraverted Anglican clergy really are. But the notion of Anglican clergy is very wide. Perhaps the population with which we are concerned should be narrowed to Anglican clergy in England (that is, the Church of England), to those who have not yet retired, to those in stipendiary ministry, to those in parochial ministry, to clergy who have been ordained at least five years, to male clergy only. Each successive delimiter helps us to become clearer about the population and about the group concerning which our research can speak with confidence.

Once the population has been defined, we can calculate just how many individuals there are in that population. If our interest really is in male Anglican clergy in England ordained at least five years and in stipendiary parochial ministry, we will recognise that we would be unlikely to be able to study them all. We need to find a sample from which we could generalise to the population. There are different sampling techniques.

A *probability or random sample* is based upon a mechanism which selects the sample by chance. The names of all the clergy could be put into a hat and pulled out at random. Or the names could be printed out in alphabetical order and every twentieth name selected to generate a 5% random sample.

A somewhat more sophisticated strategy is to use a *quota sample* which ensures that certain characteristics of the population are properly represented in the sample chosen. In the case of Anglican clergymen, a quota sample might select a fixed ratio between those chosen from the Province of York (the North) and those chosen from the Province of Canterbury (the South).

In practice, proper random samples or quota samples may be too difficult or (more likely) too expensive to obtain. For this reason, a number of studies use convenience or opportunity samples. For example, a study of Anglican clergymen might be based on those who attended a diocesan conference or a series of in-service training events. It is always important to test just how safe it is to generalise from such convenience or opportunity samples.

Response rate

The response rate is the proportion of the sample who accepted the invitation to take part in the project. When a questionnaire is handed out as part of a training event, it is likely that everyone will take part. When a questionnaire is sent out by post, the response rates can vary considerably. For example, Susan Jones' survey conducted among 672 Anglican clergy in Wales received a response rate of 82% (Jones and Francis, 1997). Mandy Robbins' survey conducted among 1,698 Anglican clergywomen in England, Ireland, Scotland, and Wales received a response rate of 73% (Francis and Robbins, 1999). Stephen Louden's survey conducted among 3,518 Roman Catholic parochial priests received a response rate of 42% (Louden and Francis, 2003).

Research ethics

Before conducting surveys like those described above, proper consideration needs to be given to ethical concerns. For example, participants need to be properly informed about the nature of the research, and given a free choice as to whether or not to participate. Attention has to be given to matters of confidentiality, anonymity and data protection procedures. The research should have no negative or harmful consequences for the participants. For further information on research ethics see, for example, Francis (1999) and Kitchener (2000).

Replication studies

Scientific knowledge remains fragmented and insecure until a body of research findings begin to cohere into producing a bigger picture. It is rather like assembling a jigsaw puzzle, seeing how the pieces can begin to fit together. But pieces of a jigsaw puzzle only fit together if they are designed to do so. One of the keys to building up knowledge in the field of faith and personality is for a group of researchers to agree on common problems, common instruments, and common research designs so that the pieces really can be made to fit together. Replication of good existing studies is all part of this programme.

Conclusion

This chapter has examined the broad issues involved in personality assessment and commended the value of a fully scientific approach to personality measurement. It has recognised that appreciation of how this scientific approach to personality works requires some basic familiarity with research methodology and with statistical tools. The aim of the next two chapters is to introduce the two different models of personality proposed by Hans Eysenck and by Raymond Cattell, before turning to the theory of psychological type in Chapter 5.

Further reading

Byrne, D (2002), *Interpreting Quantitative Data*, London, Sage.

Caprara, G V and Cervone, D (2000), *Personality: determinants, dynamics, and potentials*, Cambridge, Cambridge University Press.

Eysenck, H J and Eysenck, M W (1985), *Personality and Individual Differences: a natural science approach*, New York, Plenum Press.

Francis, L J and Robbins, M (1999), *The Long Diaconate: 1987-1994*, Leominster, Gracewing.

Francis, R D (1999), *Ethics for Psychologists: a handbook*, Leicester, British Psychological Society.

Funder, D C (1997), *The Personality Puzzle*, New York, W W Norton.

Hogan, R, Johnson, J and Briggs, S (eds) (1997), *Handbook of Personality Psychology*, London, Academic Press.

Louden, S H and Francis, L J (2003), *The Naked Parish Priest: what priests really think they're doing*, London, Continuum.

3. PERSONALITY IN THREE DIMENSIONS

Introduction

There are two long-established models of personality which have been employed in the psychology of religion both in the United States of America and in the United Kingdom for a number of years. These are the models proposed by Hans Eysenck and his associates (see Eysenck and Eysenck, 1985) and by Raymond Cattell and his associates (see Cattell, Eber and Tatsuoka, 1970). These two models are worth examination and scrutiny for two reasons.

First, the two models take very different approaches regarding what they understand by personality. Indeed the two pioneers have engaged in considerable debate regarding the relative merits of their preferred positions (see Cattell, 1986; Eysenck, 1972, 1991). Second, both models have been shown to be useful, in their own ways, for illuminating individual differences in religious faith and among the clergy. We will begin in this chapter with Eysenck's model and then turn to Cattell's model in Chapter 4. The value of the Big Five model of personality for religious research has recently been summarised by Piedmont (1999).

Reflecting on experience

Psychologists have tended to agree that the distinction between introversion and extraversion is core to profiling individual differences in personality. If you could name just two other core aspects of personality, what would you choose? Describe the two factors you have chosen and formulate reasons for your choice.

Hans Eysenck's theory

Eysenck's understanding of the structure of human personality is grounded on two fundamental assumptions, one concerning the nature of mental illness and the other concerning the independence of different dimensions of personality. Both assumptions are controversial. They have, nonetheless, led to the generation of significant insights into the nature of individual differences.

Eysenck's assumption concerning the nature of mental illness is this. He assumes a clear continuity between psychological health and psychological pathology. In other words, he envisaged no categorical distinction between normal personality and abnormal personality. Rather, the psychologically ill display a particular concentration or intensity of characteristics which are present to greater or lesser degrees in the healthy population.

Looked at in another way, for Eysenck neurotic disorders are to be identified and located at one extreme of a dimension of normal personality. This dimension extends from emotional stability at the low-scoring end of the continuum, through emotional lability, to neurotic disorder at the opposite end of the same continuum.

Similarly, for Eysenck psychotic disorders are to be identified at one extreme of another dimension of normal personality. This dimension extends from tendermindedness at the low-scoring end of the continuum, through toughmindedness, to psychotic disorder at the opposite end of the same continuum.

Eysenck's assumption concerning the independence of different dimensions of personality demands that, for example, neuroticism and psychoticism are conceptualised as totally unrelated phenomena. When Eysenck set about developing instruments to measure these dimensions of personality, he determined that the questionnaire items which assessed each dimension should show no overlap with the other dimensions. The statistical tool employed to secure this independence is provided by factor analysis.

Alongside the two independent dimensions of personality defined at the extreme high-scoring end of the continua by neurotic disorders and by psychotic disorders, Eysenck's model included the third dimension of extraversion which is unrelated to psychopathology. This dimension extends from introversion at the low-scoring end of the continuum, through ambiversion, to extraversion at the opposite end of the same continuum.

The requirement that the three major dimensions of personality should be independent from one another (or in mathematical terms, uncorrelated or orthogonal) means that knowing about someone's position on one of the dimensions cannot help predict that person's position on the other two dimensions. All three scores are therefore needed in order to locate an individual within Eysenck's three-dimensional personality space.

When Eysenck's scales are used to describe normal personality (as distinct from psychological pathology), the following three distinctions are made: between introversion and extraversion, between stability and neuroticism, and between tendermindedness and toughmindedness. Toughmindedness is generally preferred to the term psychoticism, although the term neuroticism is generally employed to describe individuals scoring in the normal range of high scores on that scale.

Individuals who record high scores within the normal range on all three scales could be described as toughminded neurotic extraverts. Individuals who record low scores on all three scales could be described as tenderminded stable introverts. All three scales, however, are designed to locate individuals on a continuum between low scores and high scores. There are no defined cutting off points according to which, for example, introverts can be separated out from extraverts. Eysenck's model does not conceive of personality measurement as locating individuals in discrete categories so much as displaying how individual differences are graded on those three dimensions.

In using Eysenck's model of personality, it is always important to compare the scores recorded by specific samples of people with the published norms provided for the same editions of the personality measure.

EXERCISE

Consider the names given to the two dimensions of personality which Eysenck sets alongside extraversion, namely neuroticism and psychoticism. How do you feel about your personality being described in terms like that? What characteristics would you expect to find in the individual who scored high on the neuroticism scale? What characteristics would you expect to find in the individual who scores high on the psychoticism scale?

Developing the dimensions

Eysenck's three-dimensional model of personality has developed over a long period. The history is important because the model has changed over time and it is confusing to piece the evidence from different studies together without knowing the story of how it all evolved.

Eysenck's earliest concern was with assessing neuroticism. His first personality test, the Maudsley Medical Questionnaire (MMQ), focused on this dimension (Eysenck, 1952). The next personality test, the Maudsley Personality Inventory (MPI), established the two-dimensional model of personality, embracing both neuroticism and extraversion (Eysenck, 1959). Following that, the Eysenck Personality Inventory (EPI) proposed more reliable and more independent measures of the same two dimensions, neuroticism and extraversion (Eysenck and Eysenck, 1964). Up to this stage Eysenck was working with a two-dimensional model of personality.

The breakthrough from two dimensions to three came with the development of the Eysenck Personality Questionnaire (EPQ) by Eysenck and Eysenck (1975). Now psychoticism was introduced to the family of dimensions, as described by Eysenck and Eysenck (1976) in their book *Psychoticism as a Dimension of Personality*. As is so often the case when a new member is introduced to a well-established family, the introduction of psychoticism has profound implications for at least one of the longerstanding dimensions of personality. In order to keep the two dimensions of psychoticism and extraversion orthogonal or uncorrelated, Eysenck had to change some of the items in the extraversion scale. Instead of being concerned with a blend of sociability and impulsivity, Eysenck's notion of extraversion settled into sociability, while the impulsivity component found a new home in the measure of psychoticism (see Rocklin and Revelle, 1981).

The most recent form of Eysenck's personality test, and the one most frequently employed in current studies, is known as the Revised Eysenck Personality Questionnaire (EPQR) first published by Eysenck, Eysenck and Barrett (1985). This test is available in a 100-item full form, a 48-item short form (EPQR-S), and a 24-item abbreviated form (EPQR-A), the latter of which was developed by Francis, Brown and Philipchalk (1992). All three versions propose measures of extraversion, neuroticism and psychoticism.

Alongside this family of tests designed for use among adults, a second family of tests was developed for use among children and young people, including the Junior Eysenck Personality Inventory (JEPI: Eysenck, 1965), the Junior Eysenck Personality Questionnaire (JEPQ: Eysenck and Eysenck, 1985), the Junior Revised Eysenck Personality Questionnaire (JEPQR: Corulla, 1990), and the abbreviated Junior Revised Eysenck Personality Questionnaire (JEPQR-A: Francis, 1996).

Since the development of the Maudsley Personality Inventory, Eysenck's tests have also included what he describes as a lie scale. The original aim of the lie scale was to detect those people who 'fake good' their personality profile, but it can also be seen to function as an index of social conformity (see Francis, 1991a). In other words, individuals who record high scores on the lie scale are more likely to follow accepted conventions, practices and values. Individuals who record low scores on the lie scale are more likely to be unconventional in their outlook.

Defining the dimensions

Having traced the ways in which Eysenck's dimensional model of personality evolved, we now turn attention to the ways in which the constructs are defined in the most recent edition of the test manual (Eysenck and Eysenck, 1991). The extravert is described in this manual as someone who is:

> sociable, likes parties, has many friends, needs to have people to talk to, and does not like reading or studying by himself. He craves excitement, takes chances, often sticks his neck out, acts on the spur of the moment, and is generally an impulsive individual. He is fond of practical jokes, always has a ready answer, and generally likes change; he is carefree, easy-going, optimistic, and likes to 'laugh and be merry'. He prefers to keep moving and doing things. (p. 4)

By way of contrast, the introvert is described as someone who is:

> a quiet, retiring sort of person, introspective, fond of books rather than people; he is reserved and distant except to intimate friends. He tends to plan ahead, 'looks before he leaps', and distrusts the impulse of the moment. He does not like excitement, takes matters of everyday life with proper seriousness, and likes a well-ordered mode of life. (p. 4)

The person who records high scores on the neuroticism scale is described as:

an anxious, worrying individual, moody and frequently depressed. He is likely to sleep badly, and to suffer from various psychosomatic disorders. He is overly emotional, reacting too strongly to all sorts of stimuli, and finds it difficult to get back on an even keel after each emotionally arousing experience. His strong emotional reactions interfere with his proper adjustment, making him react in irrational, sometimes rigid ways. (p. 4)

By way of contrast, the person who records low scores on the neuroticism scale is described as someone who:

tends to respond emotionally only slowly and generally weakly, and to return to baseline quickly after emotional arousal; he is usually calm, even-tempered, controlled and unworried. (p. 5)

The person who records high scores on the psychoticism scale is described as someone who:

may be cruel and inhumane, lacking in feeling and empathy, and altogether insensitive. He is hostile to others, even his own kith and kin, and aggressive, even to loved ones. He has a liking for odd and unusual things, and a disregard for danger; he likes to make fools of other people, and to upset them. Socialisation is a concept which is relatively alien to high P scorers; empathy, feelings of guilt, and sensitivity to other people are notions which are strange and unfamiliar to them. (p. 6)

By way of contrast, the person who records low scores on the psychoticism scale is described as someone who is empathic, unselfish, altruistic, warm, peaceful, and generally more pleasant, although possibly less socially decisive.

EXERCISE
Look carefully at the definitions which Eysenck offers for the three dimensions of personality styled extraversion, neuroticism and psychoticism and try to design some questions to include in a personality test which could tease out where people are located on each of these dimensions.

Personality and religion

There are two key questions regarding the relationship between personality and religion which have fascinated psychologists over the years (Argyle, 1958). The first question asks simply if people with some specific personality profiles are likely to be more religious than people with other personality profiles. The second question asks if there is a relationship between personality and the ways in which people express their religious faith. It is the first of these two questions which I plan to address in relation to Eysenck's dimensional model of personality.

When Argyle and Beit-Hallahmi (1975) published their classic review of empirical research in the psychology of religion, they concluded that there was, at that stage, insufficient evidence to support the view that there is a stable relationship between personality and religion. The problem was, in part, that prior to 1975 little attempt had been made to build up a secure body of empirical evidence on the relationship between personality and religion, using a recognised model of personality and a coherent index of religion. In other words, there had been a lack of replication studies which could lead to confidence in any given set of findings.

The situation has changed considerably since 1975. One of the major influences has been a considerable number of international studies which have set out to locate individual differences in religiosity within Eysenck's dimensional model of personality. A good number of these international studies have also agreed on using the Francis Scale of Attitude toward Christianity (Francis, Lewis, Philipchalk, Brown and Lester, 1995) as the way of assessing individual differences in religiosity. When Beit-Hallahmi and Argyle (1997) updated their review two decades after their earlier book, they needed to revise their conclusion. Now they concluded that the empirical research pointed to consistent and stable evidence for a relationship between personality and religion, and it was to the Eysenckian tradition that they referred. So what has been found?

EXERCISE

Thinking about Eysenck's three-dimensional model of personality, which if any of these do you imagine might be associated with people being more religious? Are extraverts likely to be more or less religious than introverts? Are neurotic individuals likely to be ▶▶

more or less religious than stable individuals? Are toughminded individuals likely to be more or less religious than tenderminded individuals? What are the grounds for your opinions?

Neuroticism and religion

Francis and his associates began their research programme in the late 1970s by concentrating first on Eysenck's dimension of neuroticism. Their original findings were published by Francis, Pearson, Carter and Kay (1981a) and then two replication studies were published by Francis, Pearson and Kay (1983a) and by Francis and Pearson (1991).

At that stage Francis and his associates were intrigued by the conflicting accounts that appeared in the psychological literature regarding the hypothesised relationship between religion and psychological health generally speaking, or between religion and neuroticism in particular. One account suggests that religion either fosters, or is an expression of, mental instability. This view could be supported by readings of Freud (1950), Ellis (1962) or Vine (1978) and predicts a positive correlation between religion and neuroticism. Sigmund Freud, in particular, is noted for believing that religion could be detrimental to mental health. The other account, however, suggests that religion fosters psychological health and mental stability. This view could be supported by readings of Jung (1938), Allport (1950) and Mowrer (1960) and predicts a negative correlation between religion and neuroticism. Carl Jung, in particular, is noted for believing that religion could be beneficial to mental health.

Francis and his associates tested out these two conflicting hypotheses on three samples of 1,088, 1,715, and 177 adolescents, each time using the Francis Scale of Attitude toward Christianity alongside different editions of Eysenck's neuroticism scale.

At first their findings seemed to suggest that there was a positive correlation between neuroticism and religion. The correlation was small, but highly significant statistically ($r = .10$, $P<.001$). But when the data were analysed more carefully this apparent relationship between neuroticism and religiosity collapsed as being entirely a consequence of sex differences. The truth of the matter is that women generally score more highly than men on the neuroticism scales (Francis, 1993). At the same time, women generally score more highly than men on indices of religiosity (Francis, 1997). Once sex differences were taken into account, the correlation between neuroticism and religion disappeared.

This lack of relationship between Eysenck's dimension of neuroticism and religion has now been confirmed by many cross-cultural studies using the Francis Scale of Attitude toward Christianity (see, for example, Francis, Lewis, Brown, Philipchalk and Lester, 1995). So the conclusion must be drawn that the personality dimension known as neuroticism is irrelevant to whether or not someone is likely to be religious.

Extraversion and religion

Francis and his associates continued their research programme by concentrating on Eysenck's dimension of extraversion. Their original findings were published by Francis, Pearson, Carter and Kay (1981b) and then two replication studies were published by Francis, Pearson and Kay (1983b), and Francis and Pearson (1985a).

This time the theory on which they built their hypothesis was provided by Siegman (1963), who based his notion on social learning theory or socialisation. According to this theory, aggressive and sexual impulses are socialised by means of conditioning into more tender-minded attitudes (which include religion), and introverts have been shown by other studies to condition more easily than extraverts (Eysenck, 1967).

In their first study Francis, Pearson, Carter and Kay (1981b) found a significant negative correlation between extraversion and religion ($r = -.15$, $P<.001$). In the second study the correlation remained significant but was much smaller ($r = -.07$, $P<.01$). In the third study the correlation dropped into insignificance. The explanation for these differences between the three studies resides in the edition of the extraversion scale used. The third study, reported by Francis and Pearson (1985a) had used the newer conceputalisation of extraversion proposed by the Eysenck Personality Questionnaire. Clearly those aspects of extraversion which had formed the relationship with religion had now been separated off from the new extraversion scale and had probably gone to join the psychoticism scale.

The lack of relationship between Eysenck's dimension of extraversion and religion has now been confirmed by many cross-cultural studies using the Francis Scale of Attitude toward Christianity. So the conclusion must be drawn that the personality dimension known as extraversion is irrelevant to whether or not someone is likely to be religious.

Psychoticism and religion

Third, Francis and his associates turned their attention to Eysenck's dimension of psychoticism. Their original findings were published by Francis and Pearson (1985b) and Francis (1992). The first of these studies, conducted among 132 15-year-olds, found significant correlations between attitude toward Christianity and the junior form of the psychoticism scale ($r + -.16$, P<.05) and the adult form of the psychoticism scale ($r = -.22$, P<.01). The second study, conducted among 1,347 14- to 16-year-olds, also found significant correlations between attitude toward Christianity and the junior form of the psychoticism scale ($r = -.33$, P<.001) and the adult form of the psychoticism scale ($r = -.30$, P<.001). These findings remained stable after taking sex differences into account.

This significant negative relationship between Eysenck's dimension of psychoticism and religion has now been confirmed by many cross-cultural studies using the Francis Scale of Attitude toward Christianity. Two different theoretical accounts have been offered for this finding. The first account builds on Eysenck's social learning theory and argues that tenderminded individuals condition more readily into religious attitudes. The second account builds on notions of psychological femininity and argues that low psychoticism scores and religiosity are consistent with psychological femininity among both men and women. What the empirical evidence shows, however, is simply that personality does make a difference to religiosity. Individuals who record low scores on the psychoticism scale are also likely to be more religious, and this holds true for men and for women.

Personality and the clergy

There are two key questions regarding the relationship between personality and the clergy which have fascinated psychologists over the years (Dittes, 1971). The first question asks simply if people with some specific personality profiles are more likely than others to be drawn into the clerical profession. The second question asks if there is a relationship between personality and the ways in which clergy express their ministry and faith. It is the first of these two questions which I plan to address in relation to Eysenck's dimensional model of personality.

> **EXERCISE**
> What predictions would you make about the personality profiles
> of clergymen and clergywomen? Would you expect clergy to be
> more or less extraverted, more or less neurotic, more or less
> toughminded, compared with men and women in general? And
> would you expect there to be significant differences across
> denominations?

When Francis (1991b) published his first main study on the personality profile of Anglican ordinands, he was able to identify a considerable body of research on the personality profiles of those engaged in
a number of professions including cartoonists (Pearson, 1983),
chartered accountants (Granleese and Barrett, 1990), commercial air-
line pilots (Evans, 1986), female nurses (Bradley, 1986), male nurses
(Gumley, McKenzie, Ormerod and Keys, 1979) and school teachers
(Innes and Kitto, 1989). But he was able to locate very little work on the
personality profile of clergy, apart from the study of Towler and Coxon
(1979) who had administered the Eysenck Personality Inventory during the mid 1960s to 76 male ordinands attending four theological col-
leges. The mean scores recorded by these ordinands on the scales of
extraversion and neuroticism are almost identical to the population
norms reported in the test manual. This early Eysenck test did not
include the psychoticism scale.

Building on Towler and Coxon's (1979) pioneering study, Francis
(1991b) administered the Eysenck Personality Questionnaire to 155
male and 97 female Anglican ordinands. Compared with Towler and
Coxon's study, here was a larger sample and a more recent version of
Eysenck's dimensional model of personality. The findings were quite
surprising.

The male ordinands emerged as significantly more introverted than
men in general. In fact their extraversion scores were closer to the
population norms for women than for men. This finding led to the
conclusion that male clergy may tend to project a feminine personality profile, at least in the Anglican Church. Certainly this would fit
with the view that the Anglican Church has become a highly feminised
environment, now much more readily accessible by women than by
men.

The female ordinands, on the other hand, emerged as significantly more extraverted than women in general. In fact their extraversion scores were closer to the population norms for men than for women. Moreover, the female ordinands were also more stable than women in general and more toughminded than women in general. In fact their neuroticism and psychoticism scores were closer to the population norms for men than for women. This finding led to the conclusion that female clergy may, at that time at least, tend to project a masculine personality profile. Certainly this would fit with the way in which in the late 1980s clergywomen were still having to adopt the pioneering stance of fighting for admission to the priesthood, which was not to come in the Church of England until 1994.

More recent studies among Anglican clergy have shown less pronounced differences between the clergymen and the clergywomen (Robbins, Francis and Rutledge, 1997).

Studies among other denominations have built on these studies among Anglican clergy. Louden and Francis (1999) reported on a sample of 1,168 Roman Catholic parochial secular priests. In terms of the two major dimensions of extraversion and neuroticism these priests displayed a personality profile more characteristic of women. In other words, Roman Catholic priests were more introverted than men in general and more neurotic than men in general. In terms of the third major dimension of psychoticism, the Roman Catholic priests displayed a clearly masculine profile.

Robbins, Francis, Haley and Kay (2001) reported on a sample of 1,102 male Methodist ministers and 237 female Methodist ministers. Their findings, too, supported the view that ministry may appeal particularly to men who value and display the tenderminded characteristics associated with femininity and to women who value and display the stable personality characteristics associated with masculinity.

The tendency for male clergy to display significantly lower extraversion scores does not extend to all denominations. The two studies reported by Francis and Kay (1995) among Pentecostal ministry candidates and by Kay (2000) among Pentecostal ministers suggest that male Pentecostal clergy are at least as extravert as men in general and possibly more so. Then the study by Francis and Robbins (2004) found that pastors associated with the New Churches are even more extraverted than those associated with the classic Pentecostal Churches.

Conclusion

This chapter has examined the three-dimensional model of personality proposed by Hans Eysenck in terms of extraversion, neuroticism and psychoticism. The model has been found to be useful in discussing the relationship between personality and religion and in examining the personality profiles of clergymen and clergywomen associated with different denominations. More research is still needed on the wider application of this model as a useful tool in practical theology. The next chapter now turns attention to the very different model of personality proposed by Raymond Cattell.

Further reading

Eysenck, H J (1990), *Rebel with a Cause: autobiography*, London, W H Allen.

Eysenck, H J and Eysenck, M W (1985), *Personality and Individual Differences: a natural science approach*, New York, Plenum Press.

Eysenck, H J and Eysenck, S B G (1976), *Psychoticism as a Dimension of Personality*, London, Hodder and Stoughton.

Eysenck, H J and Wilson, G D (1975), *Know Your Own Personality*, Harmondsworth, Penguin.

Nyborg, H (ed.) (1977), *The Scientific Study of Human Nature: tribute to Hans J Eysenck at eighty*, Oxford, Pergamon.

4. PROFILING SIXTEEN PERSONALITY FACTORS

Introduction

In some ways Hans Eysenck's approach and Raymond Cattell's approach to personality assessment have much in common. Both were committed to exploring the structure of individual differences through empirical observation and through mathematical analyses. In other ways their approaches are radically different. Eysenck concentrated on higher-order personality dimensions, while Cattell concentrated on lower-order personality traits. As a consequence, Eysenck's instruments are able to report on only three dimensions, while Cattell's instruments are generally able to report on sixteen traits. Cattell, some would argue, is as a consequence able to provide a much richer description of personality. Others maintain that Cattell's model provides unnecessary information overload.

Eysenck assumed that the major dimensions of personality were orthogonal and uncorrelated. His mathematical models forced clarity between the dimensions by rejecting personality indicators or questionnaire items which did not meet this criterion. Cattell expected his lower-order personality traits to reflect interaction one with another. Cattell, some would argue, is simply being true to the way things are. Others maintain that Cattell is simply not thinking clearly enough about the differences between his hypothesised traits.

Eysenck assumed that good personality measures needed to demonstrate a high level of internal consistency reliability (which would be reflected in high alpha coefficients). In other words, all the items in one of Eysenck's scales were designed to assess the same tightly defined domain. Cattell expected his scales to measure more broadly based constructs and so he resisted the pressures for high levels of internal homogeneity. He would see a high alpha coefficient as an indicator of a poor scale since the domain would be too tightly defined. Cattell, some would argue, has therefore developed more interesting personality constructs. Others maintain that Cattell is simply creating poor measuring instruments.

And so the debate goes on.

Reflecting on experience

Having experienced the restriction in the previous chapter of trying to discuss personality within just three major dimensions, what kind of personality traits might you want to call into play in order to describe your own personality more fully and to profile the personality of others?

Defining the factors

In order to appreciate Cattell's model of personality, it is necessary to examine each of the sixteen personality factors in turn, as proposed by the Sixteen Personality Factor Questionnaire (16PFQ: Cattell, Eber and Tatsuoka, 1970). This instrument was designed for use among adults. The factors are known by a letter or by a letter and number. Not all the letters of the alphabet are used (there is no factor D, J, K, or P), so do not be taken by surprise when some letters do not appear. The factors are then best identified by reference to the simple word descriptions of the low scoring and high scoring ends of the scale. Conventionally some brief description is then given of the high scorers and of the low scorers.

Factor A

Factor A assesses a trait from *reserved* to *outgoing*. It examines how ready people are to be warmly involved with others. High scorers on this factor are energised by their warm involvement with other people, caring for them and being concerned with their welfare. They make friends easily and devote a lot of their energy toward finding and making contacts. Being with people is their life-blood. Low scorers use less energy associating with people and therefore have more energy for pursuits which do not involve interaction with others. They may be more ideas-centred, mechanically minded, or creative.

Factor B

Factor B assesses a trait from *less intelligent* to *more intelligent*. It examines how able people are intellectually. High scorers on this factor tend to be quick to grasp ideas, and are usually fast learners. Low scorers tend to be slow to learn and to grasp new ideas. They tend to formulate concrete and literal interpretations of evidence.

Factor C

Factor C assesses a trait from *emotionally less stable* to *emotionally stable*. It examines how much people feel in control of the daily demands of life. High scorers on this factor generally feel in control of life and its demands. They adjust well to changing circumstances and do not feel bowed down by the pressures of living. They tend not to blame themselves or others for things that happen in life. Low scorers are likely to become dissatisfied with life, feeling unable to cope with its pressures and changes. They tend to lurch from one challenge to another, rather than anticipating difficulties and learning from previous experience.

Factor E

Factor E assesses a trait from *deferential* to *dominant*. It examines how much people exert influence over others. High scorers on this factor express their views and opinions strongly. They may enjoy positions of power and leadership in which they find themselves controlling other people. They tend to be rigid and somewhat aggressive if they do not get their own way. Low scorers tend to be much more influenced in their decision-making by the views and beliefs of others. They tend to be self-effacing, wishing to avoid conflict by deferring to the views of others. They lack self-confidence. They tend to be followers rather than leaders.

Factor F

Factor F assesses a trait from *serious* to *lively*. It examines how much people prefer excitement-seeking as opposed to seriousness. High scorers on this factor express themselves spontaneously. They enjoy stimulating social situations and the excitement of being at the centre of the stage. They believe in the expression, 'eat, drink and be merry!' They can throw themselves into projects with enthusiasm, but bore quickly. Low scorers have a serious, pessimistic attitude to life. They consider the implications of things carefully before speaking or acting.

Factor G

Factor G assesses a trait from *expedient* to *rule-conscious*. It examines how much people are concerned to keep the rules and regulations of their society. High scorers on this factor regard themselves as principled people. They tend to be law-abiding, self-controlled, conscientious citizens whose behaviour is guided by rules and regulations. They adhere to rules because they are there, rather than because they necessarily agree with them. Low scorers tend to be expedient and possibly rebellious. They are not socially conforming, and believe that people have the right to make their own moral and ethical choices.

Factor H

Factor H assesses a trait from *shy* to *socially bold*. It examines how much people feel at ease in social surroundings. High scorers on this factor are responsive, genial people who relish being at the centre of social situations. They are among the first to initiate social contacts between others at a party and are not reluctant to make the first move. They are not intimidated by strangers or unfamiliar situations. Low scorers are socially timid people who dislike mingling with others. They tend to avoid social groups, and prefer to stay in the background. They are emotionally cautious, preferring to stay with the predictable and to avoid risks.

Factor I

Factor I assesses a trait from *toughminded* to *sensitive*. It examines how much people prefer to make decisions on the basis of subjective feelings rather than hard data. High scorers on this factor are concerned primarily with values and emotional feelings when they are making decisions, particularly decisions which will impinge on the lives of others. They develop strong powers of empathy. Low scorers are concerned primarily with objectivity. When making decisions they rely on logical analysis of the matter in hand, rather than the consequences for other people's feelings. They tend to have little appreciation of other people's feelings and emotional needs.

EXERCISE

Look carefully at the eight factors already described: factors A, B, C, E, F, G, H and I. From what you now understand about these

▶▶

factors, where would you locate yourself: at the high-scoring end, the low-scoring end, or in the middle range? How helpful do you find these factors in discussing your own personality?

Factor L

Factor L assesses a trait from *trusting* to *vigilant*. It examines how much people question the motives behind what others say and do. High scorers on this factor are vigilant about others' intentions, questioning their motives and suspecting that things are not as they might appear. They are concerned about what others are saying behind their backs. Low scorers tend to assume that others are what they seem to be and they trust the motives of others. They relax in the presence of others, secure in the thought that they are unlikely to suffer harm or need to be on guard against some covert plan.

Factor M

Factor M assesses a trait from *practical* to *abstracted*. It examines how much people allow their attention to wander beyond the immediate situation to abstract ideas. High scorers on this factor spend much time in theoretical consideration and generation of ideas. They speculate on a variety of approaches to problems. They concentrate on the wider picture and are able to get new angles on issues. Low scorers focus their attention on the external environment of the five senses. They are keen on working out the practicalities of a project, planning its detail and gathering the necessary facts and materials.

Factor N

Factor N assesses a trait from *forthright* to *private*. It examines how much people open up to others in terms of disclosing private information about themselves. High scorers on this factor do not open up readily to others. They are personally guarded, valuing their privacy and keeping their problems to themselves. They disclose little information about themselves. Low scorers display an open, unguarded style towards other people. Self-disclosure is central to their mode of behaviour. They are spontaneous with others, talking about all aspects of their background, feelings, hopes and fears.

Factor O

Factor O assesses a trait from *self-assured* to *apprehensive*. It examines how much people worry about things, before and after the event, and how much they feel apprehensive and insecure. High scorers on this factor worry about what they say and do and about whether they come up to other people's expectations. They feel very downhearted and hurt when people criticise them, especially in front of others. Low scorers feel confident and cheerful about themselves, not worrying what other people think of them. They do not feel guilty about their actions and mistakes.

Factor Q1

Factor Q1 assesses a trait from *conservative* to *open to change*. It examines how much people are open to change and to experimentation. High scorers on this factor are continually open to new ideas and experiences. They tend to be bored by routine and repetitive tasks, preferring to pioneer new ways of doing things. Low scorers value the tradition of the past, feeling secure when they stay with familiar, well-tried methods. They are happy with routine. They are good at following the directions or instructions provided by others, but tend to be reluctant to take chances with new initiatives.

Factor Q2

Factor Q2 assesses a trait from *group-dependent* to *self-reliant*. It examines how much people prefer to do things alone, as opposed to doing things with others. High scorers on this factor prefer to do things alone. They make decisions based on their own thinking and judgements. They enjoy their own company and can cope without input from others. Low scorers desire to belong to a group and to be part of a group identity. They value the input of others in making their decisions or choices. They tend to like working with committees.

Factor Q3

Factor Q3 assesses a trait from *tolerant of disorder* to *perfectionist*. It examines how much people plan ahead in an organised fashion because they want things done correctly. High scorers on this factor are perfectionists. They have definite personal standards to which they adhere and they are reluctant to cut corners so that tasks can be finished more quickly. They are self-disciplined. Low scorers are adaptable, flexible and spontaneous. They tend to react to circumstances as they happen and are willing to suspend one activity for another. They prefer not to make irrevocable decisions too quickly.

Factor Q4

Factor Q4 assesses a trait from *relaxed* to *tense*. It examines how much people feel physically tense and irritable. High scorers on this factor experience frequent rises in their levels of physical tension, muscle tension, and emotional fatigue. They tend to feel annoyed easily by comparatively trivial incidents. An interruption at the wrong time can tip the balance into explosive tension. Low scorers tend to feel calm and tranquil. Others' actions do not make them irritable or impatient. They feel relaxed and easy-going in their work and relationships.

EXERCISE
Look carefully at the eight factors just described: factors L, M, N, O, Q1, Q2, Q3 and Q4. From what you now understand about these factors, where would you locate yourself: at the high-scoring end, the low-scoring end, or in the middle range? How helpful do you find these factors in discussing your own personality?

Childhood and adolescence

Eysenck's model of personality proposes the centrality of the same three major dimensions of personality throughout life. Hence both the Eysenck Personality Questionnaire and the Junior Eysenck Personality Questionnaire (Eysenck and Eysenck, 1975) are designed to assess the same three dimensions of extraversion, neuroticism and psychoticism.

Cattell's model of personality, however, suggests a somewhat different approach among young people. The High School Personality Questionnaire (HSPQ: Cattell, Cattell and Johns, 1984) proposes a model of fourteen factors. Twelve of these factors are basically the same as in the adult 16FP, namely factors A, B, C, E, F, G, H, I O, Q2, Q3, and Q4. Then two new factors are added, labelled D and J.

Factor D assesses a trait from *phlegmatic* to *excitable*. High scorers on this factor tend to be restless sleepers, easily distracted from work, and are hurt and angry when they are restrained or punished. They tend to be impulsive. Low scorers on this factor tend to be stoical, complacent, deliberate, self-effacing and constant. They are not easily jealous and are not given to restlessness.

Factor J assesses a trait from *vigorous* to *withdrawn*. High scorers on this factor tend to be physically and mentally fastidious, inclined to think over their mistakes and how to avoid them. They tend to feel tired when they get up in the morning. They tend to have fewer friends than most people. Low scorers on this factor tend to like attention. They go readily with the group and allow themselves to become absorbed within the group enterprise. They tend to be full of zest and given to action.

Personality and religion

Building on the work reported in the previous chapter, in which Francis and his associates set out to locate attitude toward Christianity within Eysenck's dimensional model of personality, Rosamund Bourke recently set out to conduct a similar series of studies using Cattell's model of personality. Bourke decided to base her research among secondary school pupils and used the fourteen factors proposed by the High School Personality Questionnaire (Cattell, Cattell and Johns, 1984).

Bourke's original study was conducted among a sample of 1,070 secondary school pupils between the ages of eleven and eighteen years (Francis and Bourke, 2004). In order to check the findings from their original study, Bourke conducted a replication, this time among 845 secondary school pupils between the ages of thirteen and fifteen years (Bourke, Francis and Robbins, 2004). The two studies produced almost exactly the same pattern of relationships with the fourteen personality factors, enabling us to have some confidence in the findings. Clearly further replication studies would be desirable, but a good start has already been made.

On the one hand, no significant relationship was found between attitude toward Christianity and nine of Cattell's fourteen factors. According to factor A, religious young people were neither more reserved nor more outgoing. According to factor B, religious young people were neither less intelligent nor more intelligent. According to factor C, religious young people were neither emotionally less stable nor emotionally more stable. According to Factor D, religious young people were neither more phlegmatic nor more excitable. According to factor H, religious young people were neither more shy nor more venturesome.

According to factor J, religious young people were neither more vigorous nor more withdrawn. According to factor O, religious young people were neither more self-assured nor more apprehensive. According to factor Q2, religious young people were neither more group-dependent nor more self-sufficient. According to factor Q4, religious young people were neither more relaxed nor more tense.

On the other hand, a significant relationship was found between attitude toward Christianity and five of Cattell's factors: factors E, F, G, I and Q3. In order to consider the meaning of these findings, it is helpful to report the actual correlations found by Bourke's second study and to examine the definitions of the factors.

Factor E reported a significant negative correlation with attitude toward Christianity (r = -.29, P<.001). This means that religious young people recorded lower scores on the scale. According to Cattell's definitions, they were more likely to be characterised as deferential rather than as dominant. Religious young people tend to be more influenced in their decision-making by the views and beliefs of others. They tend to be more self-effacing, and more likely to avoid conflict by deferring to the views of others. They are more likely to lack self-confidence. They tend, overall, to be followers rather than leaders.

Factor F reported a significant negative correlation with attitude toward Christianity (r = -.21, P<.001). This means that religious young people recorded lower scores on this scale. According to Cattell's definitions, they were more likely to be characterised as serious than as lively. Religious young people tend to take a more serious approach to life. They may also tend to be more pessimistic about life. They are more likely to want to consider the implication of things carefully before speaking or acting.

Factor G reported a significant positive correlation with attitude toward Christianity (r = .32, P<.001). This means that religious young people recorded higher scores on this scale. According to Cattell's definitions, they were more likely to be characterised as rule-conscious than as expedient. Religious young people tend to regard themselves as holding to principles. They tend to be law-abiding, self-controlled and conscientious. Their behaviour tends to be guided by rules.

Factor I reported a significant positive correlation with attitude toward Christianity (r = .21, P<.001). This means that religious young people recorded higher scores on this scale. According to Cattell's definitions, they were more likely to be characterised as sensitive than as toughminded. Religious young people are more concerned with values and with feelings when they are making decisions, particularly decisions which will impinge on the lives of others. They tend to develop stronger powers of empathy.

Factor Q3 reported a significant positive correlation with attitude toward Christianity ($r = .11$, $P<.001$). This means that religious young people recorded higher scores on this scale. According to Cattell's definitions, they were more likely to be characterised as perfectionist than as tolerant of disorder. Religious young people tend to be perfectionists. They tend to have definite personal standards to which they adhere. They tend to be reluctant to cut corners so that tasks can be finished more quickly. They are self-disciplined.

EXERCISE
Look back over the findings from Bourke's studies regarding the personality profile of young people who are more religious. What do you see as the main strengths and weaknesses of religious young people in terms of Cattell's model?

Personality and the clergy

Building on the work reported in the previous chapter, in which Francis and his associates set out to describe the personality profile of clergy in terms of Eysenck's dimensional model of personality, David Musson set out to conduct a similar series of studies using Cattell's model of personality.

Musson's first two studies reported on the personality profile of 441 male Anglican clergy of the Church of England (Musson, 1998) and then compared these male clergy with 55 female clergy of the Church of England (Francis and Musson, 1999). He employed the well-established form of Cattell's measure known as the 16PF (Cattell, Eber and Tatsuoka, 1970). His sample was provided by clergy who attended residential ministry workshops. Although not a random sample, Musson's data provided at the time the best information then available on clergy personality profile based on Cattell's theory.

Subsequently, Musson established a 7% random sample of the male Anglican stipendiary clergy of the Church of England. A 60% response rate produced 332 replies (Musson, 2001). A second 50% sample of the female stipendiary clergy of the Church of England produced a response rate of 64% and 250 replies (Musson, 2002). This time he used the more recent edition of Cattell's instrument, the 16PF5 (Cattell, Cattell and Cattell, 1993). In reporting his findings, Musson decided not to use factor B, the measure of intelligence, and limited his description to the other fifteen factors.

In his random sample, Musson identified only three of these fifteen factors in which male Anglican clergy did not score significantly differently from British men in general. No differences were found between male clergy and men in general in terms of factor C (a trait from emotionally less stable to emotionally stable), factor H (a trait from shy to socially bold), and factor Q2 (a trait from group-dependent to self-reliant).

Male clergy scored significantly higher on factor A, indicating that they were more outgoing and less reserved than men in general. This is consistent with the view that clergy need to be people-centred in a pastoral ministry that endeavours to stand alongside others in their need as well as actively recruit new adherents through warm, personal contact.

Male clergy scored significantly lower on factor E, indicating that they were more deferential and less dominant than men in general. This is consistent with the fact that, in working with volunteers, clergy need to be accommodating to other people's perspectives and appreciative of efforts made in the service of the church.

Male clergy scored significantly lower on factor F, indicating that they were more serious and less lively than men in general. This is consistent with the idea that clergy display a serious, cautious attitude to life, thinking carefully before they speak and generally holding back from spontaneity.

Male clergy scored significantly higher on factor G, indicating that they were more rule-conscious and less expedient than men in general. This is consistent with the idea that clergy are themselves both under authority and the guardians of moral behaviour.

Male clergy scored particularly high on factor I, indicating that they were much more sensitive and much less toughminded than men in general. This is consistent with emotional sensitivity being core to such roles as counselling and pastoral visiting.

Male clergy scored particularly low on factor L, indicating that they were much more trusting and much less vigilant than men in general. This is consistent with the view that clergy see goodness and sincerity in others and generally perceive people as trustworthy.

Male clergy scored significantly higher on factor M, indicating that they were more abstracted and less practical than men in general. This is consistent with the view that clergy focus on what is beyond the present, and are more concerned with ideas and concepts than with practical details.

Male clergy scored significantly lower on factor N, indicating that they were more forthright and less private than men in general. This is consistent with the view that clergy are comfortable disclosing personal information about their lives and faith-journeys rather than maintaining personal privacy.

Male clergy scored significantly higher on factor O, indicating that they were more apprehensive and less self-assured than men in general. This is consistent with the view that clergy experience low levels of self-confidence and are keen to gain the approval of parishioners.

Male clergy scored significantly higher on factor Q1, indicating that they were more open to change and less conservative than men in general. This is consistent with the view that clergy are receptive to new ideas and willing to change their methods to improve their ministries.

Male clergy scored significantly lower on factor Q3, indicating that they were more tolerant of disorder and less perfectionist than men in general. This is consistent with the view that clergy often need to be reactive to situations that arise in ministry, having to handle unexpected needs and demands from their parishioners.

Male clergy scored significantly lower on factor Q4, indicating that they were more relaxed and less tense than men in general. This is consistent with the view that clergy need to handle complex human situations and emotions without letting them have negative implications for their own health and wellbeing.

Musson's subsequent comparison of the profiles of male and female clergy confirmed the findings of studies using other measures that some of the expected gender differences between men and women are actually reversed among the clergy. Contrary to the usual sex differences in personality profile found in the general population, female clergy were shown to be less outgoing (factor A), more emotionally stable (factor C), more dominant (factor E), less rule conscious (factor G), less emotionally sensitive (factor I), less apprehensive (factor O), and more open to change (Q1) than male clergy.

> **EXERCISE**
> Look back over the findings of Musson's studies regarding the personality profile of male clergy. What do you see to be the main strengths and weaknesses of male clergy in terms of Cattell's model?

Conclusion

This chapter has examined the sixteen-factor model of personality proposed by Raymond Cattell. The model has been found to be useful in discussing the relationship between personality and religion and in examining the personality profiles of clergymen and clergywomen. Once again more research is still needed on the wider application of this model as a useful tool in practical theology. The next chapter now turns attention to a third very different model of personality proposed by psychological type.

Further reading

Cattell, R B (1973), *Personality and Mood by Questionnaire*, San Francisco, California, Jossey-Bass.

Cattell, R B (1990), 'Advances in Cattellian personality theory', in L A Pervin (ed.), *Handbook on Personality: theory and research*, pp. 101-110, New York, Guildford Press.

Cattell, R B, Cattell, M D L and Johns E F (1984), *Manual and Norms for the High School Personality Questionnaire: the HSPQ*, Champaign, Illinois, Institute for Personality and Ability Testing.

Cattell, R B, Eber, H W and Tatsuoka, M M (1970), *Handbook for the Sixteen Personality Factor Questionnaire (16PF)*, Champaign, Illinois, Institute for Personality and Ability Testing.

Cattell, R B and Kline, P (1977), *The Scientific Analysis of Personality and Motivation*, London, Academic Press.

5. KNOWING YOUR PSYCHOLOGICAL TYPE

Introduction

Chapter 5 takes a very different approach from that of the previous four chapters. The previous four chapters set out to introduce broad issues concerned with the relationship between psychology and theology, with the ways in which psychology approaches the problem of human personality, and with the nature of the two models of personality proposed by Hans Eysenck and by Raymond Cattell. These chapters began with theory in order to set a wider context for further exploration.

Chapter 5 now turns attention in much greater depth to the model of personality which is going to form the basis for the rest of this book, the idea of psychological type proposed by Carl Jung and described in his book, *Psychological Types* (Jung, 1971). Instead of beginning with theory, however, our explanation of psychological type begins with experience. This chapter invites you to get to know your own psychological type, both by filling in a questionnaire and by self-exploration.

Reflecting on experience
When have you filled in personality tests in the past or completed any other form of psychological tests, like intelligence tests, or aptitude inventories? How do you feel about such instruments? What are your hopes or fears about exploring your own psychological type?

There are two key ideas which make psychological type theory very different from the two theories discussed in Chapters 3 and 4. I will emphasise these two differences by contrasting psychological type theory with Eysenck's dimensional model of personality.

Type categories

The first important characteristic of type theory concerns the distinction between psychological type categories and personality dimensions or continua. For example, Eysenck characterises introversion and extraversion as two ends of a single continuum. Eysenck's extraversion scale functions like a metre ruler or a thermometer. Individuals can be placed anywhere on that continuum. On that continuum, there is no central cut-off point which can distinguish whether you fit as an introvert or as an extravert. Individuals are simply compared one with another as scoring higher or lower on this continuum.

Jung's notion of introversion and extraversion, however, is one of two distinct types. According to Jung's theory, it is possible to categorise an individual either as an introvert or as an extravert. Ease of classification depends on levels of self-awareness and clarity of preference.

EXERCISE
Take out a piece of paper and write your signature. Do it quickly and before you read on.

Having written your signature, now pass the pen to the other hand and try again. What is the difference? How do you account for the difference? What have you learnt about yourself from this experience?

One way of looking at Jung's model of psychological type is by comparing it with our experience of handedness. We are all generally equipped with two hands, but we instinctively prefer one over the other. Consequently we develop more skills with our preferred hand and, at the same time, neglect to develop the less preferred hand to its full potential. If we were to try to take notes, say in a lecture or in a sermon, with our less preferred hand, we would notice three things. It would take a lot more concentration and make it less easy for us to listen to what is being said. It would be slower to write and much less easy to read. It would be much more tiring and draining on our energy resources.

Just as we all generally benefit from a right hand and a left hand, Jung suggests that we are all equipped with the ability to use extraversion and to use introversion. But we instinctively prefer one over the other. Consequently we develop more skills with our preferred orientation (either extraversion or introversion) and at the same time neglect to develop the less preferred orientation to its full potential.

There are lots of reasons why some people operate outside their preferred mode for much of their life. There was a time when children were all encouraged (or forced) at school to write with the right hand, irrespective of their instinctive preference. For some this seems to lead to illegible handwriting, and for others to more serious malfunctioning. There are lots of reasons, too, why some people as they are growing up are encouraged (or forced) to operate outside their preferred orientation.

Sometimes as soon as young introverts are taken to the nursery school they begin to learn that it is wise to speak out and to pretend to be an extravert in order to get noticed. Some primary schools prefer extraverted behaviour and encourage it.

Sometimes if young extraverts are growing up in a predominantly introverted household, they begin to learn that it is wise to keep quiet and to pretend to be an introvert in order to keep out of sight and out of trouble. Some homes prefer introverted behaviour and encourage it.

In such cases it may not be until considerably later in life that suppressed introverts or suppressed extraverts discover who they really are and claim their true psychological preference. The problem about living out-of-type is that it can be an inefficient use of energy resources and sometimes quite debilitating. In some of his writings Jung speaks about the *persona* or the mask which people choose to wear (or which they put on unknowingly) and behind which the real self withers. The joy about studying psychological type theory is that it sometimes helps us to see more clearly and to claim our true identity.

Type acceptance

The second important characteristic of type theory concerns the distinction between healthy personality and unhealthy personality. For example, Eysenck builds his model of personality around key concepts of psychological pathology, namely neuroticism and psychoticism. Very high scorers on Eysenck's neuroticism scale or on Eysenck's psychoticism scale may well begin to wonder about their psychological health and about their normal levels of psychological functioning.

Jung's notion of psychological type, however, is totally benign. Neither the language nor the concepts of psychological type theory have anything to do with psychological pathology. Learning about your psychological type is a completely non-threatening experience. There is nothing to fear from completing a psychological test concerned with type theory.

Assessing psychological type

Sometimes the mistake is made of equating psychological type theory exclusively with one of the better known tools designed for assessing psychological type, namely the Myers-Briggs Type Indicator (MBTI), as developed by Myers, McCaulley, Quenk and Hammer (1998) and by Kendall (1998). There are in fact a number of other instruments which have also been designed to assess Jung's original notion of psychological type, including the Keirsey Temperament Sorter (KTS) proposed by Keirsey and Bates (1978) and revised by Keirsey (1998), the Gray-Wheelwright Jungian Type Survey (Gray and Wheelwright, 1946), the Singer-Loomis Inventory of Personality (Loomis, 1982), the Personality Style Inventory (Ware, Yokomoto and Morris, 1985), the Type Differentiation Indicator (Mitchell, 1991), the Cambridge Type Inventory (Rawling, 1992), the PET Check (Cranton and Knoop, 1995), the Jung Type Indicator (Budd, 1997), and the Personal Preferences Self-Description Questionnaire (Kier, Melancon and Thompson, 1998). The most recent instrument to be added to this growing family of tests is the Francis Psychological Type Scales (FPTS) developed by Francis (2004b).

This long list of instruments has been provided to emphasise just how much broader this chapter is than a discussion of the MBTI. The instrument which you will soon be invited to complete is not the MBTI and it does not claim to act as a proxy for the MBTI. Readers who are specifically interested in learning their MBTI type are urged to contact a qualified MBTI practitioner and to complete one of the current tests sold by MBTI-licensed publishers.

EXERCISE
Turn now to the Appendix where you will find a copy of the Francis Psychological Type Scales. Find a quiet space away from
▶▶

other people and answer the questions. Work through the items systematically and quite quickly. Do not ponder for too long over any individual item. Often it is your immediate response that gets closer to the truth. Remember that there are no trick questions. When you have completed the questionnaire, carry on with the rest of this chapter. You will be invited to examine your results later.

Introducing the theory

Jung's theory of psychological type begins with the two constructs which we have already introduced: *introversion* (I) and *extraversion* (E). In Jung's theory introversion and extraversion are best characterised as two *orientations*. According to the theory, the introvert looks inwards for psychological energy, while the extravert looks outwards for psychological energy.

Then at the heart of Jung's theory stand two main psychological processes. The first psychological process concerns the ways in which we gather information. This is the *perceiving* process. In terms of the perceiving process, some people prefer *sensing* (S), while others prefer *intuition* (N). According to the theory, these two types look at the world in very different ways.

The second psychological process concerns the ways in which we make decisions. This is the *judging* process. In terms of the judging process, some people prefer *thinking* (T), while others prefer *feeling* (F). According to the theory, these two types come to decisions about the world in very different ways.

Jung's theory suggests that we prefer to use one of these processes in the outer world and the other process in the inner world. In other words, some people prefer to use judging in the outer world and to use perceiving in the inner world, while other people prefer to use judging in the inner world and to use perceiving in the outer world. Many of those who have built on Jung's theory of psychological type have proposed, therefore, a fourth indicator, often characterised as *attitude toward the outer world*. In terms of attitude toward the outer world, some people prefer to use *judging* (J) and others prefer to use *perceiving* (P). These two types present very different images to the outer world.

At this point it is important to draw attention to the very distinctive ways in which Jung uses the words *judging* and *perceiving*. Both words need to be used in the technical ways they have been defined above. *Judging* has nothing to do with being judgemental. *Perceiving* has nothing to do with being perceptive.

Having given a very brief introduction to the two orientations (introversion and extraversion), the two perceiving processes (sensing and intuition), the two judging processes (thinking and feeling) and the two attitudes to the outer world (judging and perceiving), we will introduce each in greater depth.

Introversion and extraversion

Introversion and extraversion describe the two preferred orientations of the inner world and the outer world. Introverts prefer to focus their attention on the inner world of ideas and draw their energy from that inner world. When introverts are tired and need energising they look to the inner world. Extraverts prefer to focus their attention on the outer world of people and things and draw their energy from that outer world. When extraverts are tired and need energising they look to the outer world. Since this introduction is being written by an introvert, the author prefers to present this perspective first, followed by the extravert perspective.

Introverts like quiet for concentration. They want to be able to shut off the distractions of the outer world and turn inwards. They often experience trouble in remembering names and faces. They can work at one solitary project for a long time without interruption. When they are engaged in a task in the outer world they may become absorbed in the ideas behind that task.

Introverts work best alone and may resent distractions and interruptions from other people. They dislike being interrupted by the telephone, tend to think things through before acting, and may spend so long in thought that they miss the opportunity to act.

Introverts prefer to learn by reading rather than by talking with others. They may also prefer to communicate with others in writing, rather than face-to-face or over the phone; this is particularly the case if they have something unpleasant to communicate.

Introverts are oriented to the inner world. They focus on ideas, concepts and inner understanding. They are reflective, may consider deeply before acting, and they probe inwardly for stimulation.

Extraverts like variety and action. They want to be able to shut off the distractions of the inner world and turn outward. They are good at remembering faces and names and enjoy meeting people and introducing people. They can become impatient with long, slow jobs. When they are working in the company of other people they may become more interested in how others are doing the job than in the job itself.

Extraverts like to have other people around them in the working environment, and enjoy the stimulus of sudden interruptions and telephone calls. Extraverts like to act quickly and decisively, even when it is not totally appropriate to do so.

Extraverts prefer to learn a task by talking it through with other people. They prefer to communicate with other people face-to-face or over the phone, rather than in writing. They often find that their own ideas become clarified through communicating them with others. Extraverts are oriented to the outer world. They focus on people and things. They prefer to learn by trial and error and they do so with confidence. They are active people, and they scan the outer environment for stimulation.

EXERCISE

Read through the above description of introversion and extraversion with care. Which of these descriptions provides the better account of your own preferences? Now describe your own psychological type in terms of extraversion *or* introversion.

Sensing and intuition

Sensing and intuition describe the two preferences associated with the *perceiving process*.

They describe different preferences used to acquire information. Sensing types focus on the realities of a situation as perceived by the senses. Intuitive types focus on the possibilities, meanings and relationships, the 'big picture' that goes beyond sensory information. Since this introduction is being written by an intuitive type, the author prefers to present this perspective first, followed by the sensing perspective.

Individuals who prefer *intuition* develop insight into complexity. They have the ability to see abstract, symbolic and theoretical relationships, and the capacity to see future possibilities. They put their reliance on inspiration rather than on past experience. Their interest is in the new and untried. They trust their intuitive grasp of meanings and relationships.

Individuals with a preference for intuition are aware of new challenges and possibilities. They see quickly beyond the information they have been given or the materials they have to hand to the possibilities and challenges which these offer. They are often discontent with the way things are and wish to improve them. They become bored quickly and dislike doing the same thing repeatedly.

Intuitive types enjoy learning new skills. They work in bursts of energy, powered by enthusiasm, and then enjoy slack periods between activity.

Intuitive types follow their inspirations and hunches. They may reach conclusions too quickly and misconstrue the information or get the facts wrong. They dislike taking too much time to secure precision.

Intuitive types may tend to imagine that things are more complex than they really are: they tend to over-complexify things. They are curious about why things are the way they are and may prefer to raise questions than to find answers.

Intuitive types are always striving to gain an overview of the information around them. In terms of an old proverb, they may prefer to pay attention to the two birds in the bush rather than the one in the hand.

Intuitive types perceive with memory and associations. They see patterns and meanings and assess possibilities. They are good at reading between the lines and projecting possibilities for the future. They prefer to go always for the big picture. They prefer to let the mind inform the eyes.

Individuals who prefer *sensing* develop keen awareness of present experience. They have acute powers of observation, good memory for facts and details, the capacity for realism, and the ability to see the world as it is. They rely on experience rather than theory. They put their trust in what is known and in the conventional.

Individuals with a preference for sensing are aware of the uniqueness of each individual event. They develop good techniques of observation and they recognise the practical way in which things work now.

Sensing types like to develop an established way of doing things and gain enjoyment from exercising skills which they have already learnt.

Repetitive work does not bore them. They are able to work steadily with a realistic idea of how long a task will take.

Sensing types usually reach their conclusion step by step, observing each piece of information carefully. They are not easily inspired to interpret the information in front of them and they may not trust inspiration when it comes. They are very careful about getting the facts right and are good at engaging with detail.

Sensing types may fail to recognise complexity in some situations, and consequently over-simplify tasks. They are good at accepting the current reality as the given situation in which to work. They would much rather work with the present information than speculate about future possibilities. They clearly agree with the old proverb that the bird in the hand is worth two in the bush.

Sensing types perceive clearly with the five senses. They attend to practical and factual details, and they are in touch with physical realities. They attend to the present moment and prefer to confine their attention to what is said and done. They observe the small details of everyday life and attend to step-by-step experience. They prefer to let the eyes tell the mind.

EXERCISE
Read through the above description of sensing and intuition with care. Which of these descriptions provides the better account of your own preferences? Now describe your own psychological type in terms of sensing *or* intuition.

Thinking and feeling

Thinking and feeling describe the two preferences associated with the *judging process*. They describe different preferences by which decisions are reached. Individuals who prefer thinking make decisions based on objective, logical analysis. Individuals who prefer feeling make decisions by subjective values based on how people will be affected. Since this introduction is being written by a thinking type, the author prefers to present this perspective first, followed by the feeling perspective.

Individuals who prefer *thinking* develop clear powers of logical analysis. They develop the ability to weigh facts objectively and to predict consequences, both intended and unintended. They develop a stance of impartiality. They are characterised by a sense of fairness and justice.

Individuals with a preference for thinking are good at putting things in logical order. They are able to put people in their place when they consider it necessary. They are able to take tough decisions and to reprimand others. They are also able to be firm and toughminded about themselves.

Thinking types need to be treated fairly and to see that other people are treated fairly as well. They are inclined to respond more to other people's ideas than to other people's feelings. They may inadvertently hurt other people's feelings without recognising that they are doing so.

Thinking types are able to anticipate and predict the logical outcomes of other people's choices. They can see the humour rather than the human pain in bad choices and wrong decisions taken by others. Thinking types prefer to look at life from the outside as a spectator.

Thinking types are able to develop good powers of critical analysis. They use objective and impersonal criteria in reaching decisions. They follow logically the relationships between cause and effect. They develop characteristics of being firm-minded and prizing logical order. They may appear sceptical.

Individuals who prefer *feeling* develop a personal emphasis on values and standards. They appreciate what matters most to themselves and what matters most to other people. They develop an understanding of people, a wish to affiliate with people and a desire for harmony. They are characterised by their capacity for warmth, and by qualities of empathy and compassion.

Individuals with a preference for feeling like harmony and will work hard to bring harmony about between other people. They dislike telling other people unpleasant things or reprimanding other people. They take into account other people's feelings.

Feeling types need to have their own feelings recognised as well. They need praise and affirmation. They are good at seeing the personal effects of choices on their own lives and on other people's lives as well.

Feeling types are sympathetic individuals. They take a great interest in the people behind the job and respond to other people's values as much as to their ideas. They enjoy pleasing people.

Feeling types look at life from the inside. They live life as committed participants and find it less easy to stand back and to form an objective view of what is taking place.

Feeling types develop good skills at applying personal priorities. They are good at weighing human values and motives, both their own and other people's. They are characterised by qualities of empathy and sympathy. They prize harmony and trust.

EXERCISE
Read through the above description of thinking and feeling with care. Which of these descriptions provides the better account of your own preferences? Now describe your own psychological type in terms of thinking *or* feeling.

Judging and perceiving

Judging and perceiving describe the two preferred attitudes toward the outer world. Individuals who prefer to relate to the outer world with a judging process present a planned and orderly approach to life. They prefer to have a settled system in place and display a preference for closure. Individuals who prefer to relate to the outer world with a perceiving process present a flexible and spontaneous approach to life. They prefer to keep plans and organisations to a minimum and display a preference for openness. Since this introduction is being written by a judging type, the author prefers to present this perspective first, followed by the perceiving perspective.

Judging types schedule projects so that each step gets done on time. They like to get things finished and settled, and to know that the finished product is in place. They work best when they can plan their work in advance and follow that plan. Judging types use lists and agendas to structure their day and to plan their actions. They may dislike interruption from the plans they have made and are reluctant to leave the task in hand even when something more urgent arises.

Judging types tend to be satisfied once they reach a judgement or have made a decision, both about people and things. They dislike having to revise their decision and taking fresh information into account. They like to get on with a task as soon as possible once the essential things are at hand. As a consequence, judging types may decide to act too quickly.

When individuals take a judging attitude toward the outer world, they are using the preferred *judging process*, thinking or feeling, outwardly. Their attitude to life is characterised by deciding and planning, organising and scheduling, controlling and regulating. Their life is goal-oriented. They want to move toward closure, even when the data are incomplete.

Perceiving types adapt well to changing situations. They make allowances for new information and for changes in the situation in which they are living or acting. They may have trouble making decisions, feeling that they have never quite got enough information on which to base their decision.

Perceiving types may start too many projects and consequently have difficulty in finishing them. They may tend to postpone unpleasant tasks and to give their attention to more pleasant options. Perceiving types want to know all about a new task before they begin it, and may prefer to postpone something while they continue to explore the options.

When perceiving types use lists they do so not as a way of organising the details of their day, but of seeing the possibilities in front of them. They may choose never to act on these possibilities. Perceiving types do not mind leaving things open for last minute changes. They work best under pressure and get a lot accomplished at the last minute under the constraints of a deadline.

When individuals take a perceiving attitude toward the outer world, they are using the preferred *perceiving process*, sensing or intuition, outwardly. They are taking in information, adapting and changing, curious and interested. They adopt an open-minded attitude toward life and resist closure to obtain more data.

EXERCISE
Read through the above description of judging and perceiving with care. Which of these descriptions provides the better account of your own psychological preferences? Now describe your own psychological type in terms of judging *or* perceiving.

Conclusion

This chapter has introduced Jung's theory of psychological type and provided an opportunity for you to reflect on how your own personality fits into that model. The next two chapters now examine type theory and the assessment of psychological type in greater depth.

Further reading

Goldsmith, M and Wharton, M (1993), *Knowing Me – Knowing You*, London, SPCK.

Jung, C G (1971), *Psychological Types: the collected works, volume 6*, London, Routledge and Kegan Paul.

Keirsey, D (1998), *Please Understand Me: 2*, Del Mar, California, Prometheus Nemesis.

Kroeger, O and Thuesen, J M (1988), *Type Talk*, New York, Delta.

Moore, R L (ed.) (1988), *Carl Jung and Christian Spirituality*, Mahwah, New Jersey, Paulist Press.

Moss, S (1989), *Jungian Typology*, Melbourne, Victoria, Collins Dove.

Myers, I B and Myers, P B (1980), *Gifts Differing*, Palo Alto, California, Consulting Psychologists Press.

Myers, I B and Myers, P B (1995), *Gifts Differing: understanding personality type*, Palo Alto, California, Davies-Black.

Thorne, A and Gough, H (1991), *Portraits of Type*, Palo Alto, California, Consulting Psychologists Press.

6. MEASURING AND ASSESSING PSYCHOLOGICAL TYPE

Introduction

Chapter 5 invited you to explore your own psychological type in two ways. First, before you had been introduced to the more detailed definitions of the two orientations, the two perceiving functions, the two judging functions, and the two attitudes toward the outer world, you were invited to complete the Francis Psychological Type Scales. At that stage, however, no clues were given as to how to interpret or score that questionnaire. Second, after being introduced to the definitions used in psychological type theory, you were invited to signal your own preference between the four pairs of opposites: between introversion and extraversion, between sensing and intuition, between thinking and feeling, and between judging and perceiving.

Chapter 6 now invites you to score your completed questionnaire and to compare what the questionnaire says about your psychological type preferences with the assessments you made when invited to formulate your own preferences in Chapter 5. For some people, the questionnaire will lead to exactly the same set of four preferences as the choices you made in Chapter 5. For other people there may be some significant differences between the solutions proposed by the two methods. This chapter will then go on to examine how and why such differences occur and to discuss some of the problems involved in assessing psychological type. So please do not be alarmed if the scores you record on the indicator do not immediately make sense to you!

Reflecting on experience

Revisit the four choices you made in Chapter 5 between extraversion (E) and introversion (I), between sensing (S) and intuition (N), between thinking (T) and feeling (F), and between judging (J) and perceiving (P). Write out your self-identified type, in the same form as I write mine. My preferences are for introversion, intuition, thinking and judging, or INTJ. Now try to assess your clarity about these preferences, taking a ten-point scale, from one (low clarity) to ten (high clarity). For example, I am very clear about my preference for introversion over extraversion, but much less clear about my preference for judging over perceiving. So I would choose I (10), N (5), T (4) and J (2). How easy did you find it to assess the clarity of your preferences?

Francis Psychological Type Scales

The Francis Psychological Type Scales were designed to present ten pairs of items to differentiate each of the four choices between extraversion and introversion, between sensing and intuition, between thinking and feeling, and between judging and perceiving. The four sets of ten items were then jumbled up so that the purpose behind each pair of items was not too transparent.

Our task now is to unscramble the pairs of items so that we can see more clearly how the test works and so that you can complete your scores. Each set of items will now be taken in turn.

EXERCISE

Find the pairs of items in the Francis Psychological Type Scales which are listed in Table 6.1. Where you have placed a tick in the box against the response, enter the value 1 in Table 6.1. Where you have left the box blank, enter the value 0. These are the items designed to differentiate between preferences for extraversion and for introversion. Now add up the two columns. The higher of the two scores indicates your psychological preference and the difference between the two scores indicates the clarity of your preference between extraversion and introversion. If

▸▸

both columns add up to five, then count yourself as preferring introversion. On this occasion do your self-assessment from Chapter 5 and the indicator agree or disagree? What do you learn about yourself from this?

TABLE 6.1 Orientation

extraversion		introversion
active	or	reflective
sociable	or	private
having many friends	or	a few deep friendships
likes parties	or	dislikes parties
energised by others	or	drained by too many people
happier working in groups	or	happier working alone
socially involved	or	socially detached
talkative	or	reserved
an extravert	or	an introvert
speak before thinking	or	think before speaking
Total E score		**Total I score**

Introversion and extraversion

If you are still puzzled about your real preference between introversion and extraversion, a very good test is to examine what makes you tired and then how you react when you are feeling tired.

For introverts (like the author) it is the outer world of people which makes them really tired and which can do so quite quickly. When introverts spend a full day working with people and talking with others, they will go home worn out, exhausted and puzzled as to how extraverts keep going in the company of others. In fact, at the end of such a day extraverts seem even more full of life than when the day started.

For extraverts it is the inner world of ideas and thoughts which makes them really tired and which can do so quite quickly. When extraverts spend a full day working with books and writing alone, they will go home worn out, exhausted and puzzled as to how introverts keep going in their own company. In fact, at the end of such a day introverts seem even more full of life than when the day started.

At the end of a tiring day there is nothing introverts want to do more than to go home, close the door, and be on their own. They re-energise and re-charge their batteries by being on their own.

At the end of a tiring day there is nothing extraverts want to do more than to go out and to enjoy the company of others. They re-energise and recharge their batteries by being with other people.

Given such a fundamental difference between introverts and extraverts, it is not surprising that they can sometimes easily misunderstand each other. On the one hand, extraverts may experience introverts as people who are withdrawn, aloof and very difficult to get to know. On the other hand, introverts may experience extraverts as people who are shallow and lacking in any real depth. The truth of the matter is that introverts and extraverts present themselves to the world in very different ways.

However, once they get to know and to respect each other's individuality, extraverts and introverts can complement each other's skills and perspectives on life. Introverts can benefit from extraverts in many ways. For example, extraverts can:

• help introverts to make their views known in discussions;
• help introverts to get to know other people;
• help introverts to become better known by other people;
• keep the conversation flowing in social encounters;
• break the ice in social situations.

Similarly, extraverts can benefit from introverts in many ways too. For example, introverts can:

• help extraverts to explore their own inner depths;
• provide concentration and depth on shared tasks;
• help extraverts to deal with solitude and to value it;
• enable extraverts to listen to what is going on inside themselves;
• help extraverts to listen to others;
• encourage extraverts when the going is slow and tedious.

EXERCISE
Find the pairs of items in the Francis Psychological Type Scales which are listed in Table 6.2. Where you have placed a tick in the ▶▶

box against the response, enter the value 1 in Table 6.2. Where you have left the box blank, enter the value 0. These are the items designed to differentiate between preferences for sensing and for intuition. Now add up the two columns. The higher of the two scores indicates your psychological preference and the difference between the two scores indicates the clarity of your preference between sensing and intuition. If both columns add up to five, then count yourself as preferring intuition. On this occasion do your self-assessment in Chapter 5 and the indicator agree or disagree? What do you learn about yourself from this?

TABLE 6.2 Perceiving process

sensing		intuition
interested in facts	or	interested in theories
practical	or	inspirational
the concrete	or	the abstract
prefer to make	or	prefer to design
conventional	or	inventive
concerned about detail	or	concerned for meaning
sensible	or	imaginative
present realities	or	future possibilities
keep things as they are	or	improve things
down to earth	or	up in the air
Total S score		**Total N score**

Sensing and intuition

If you are still puzzled about your real preference between sensing and intuition, a very good test is to examine how you react when you are feeling tired. It is your less preferred function which is most likely to let you down.

For intuitive types (like the author) it is the less preferred function of sensing which lets them down when they are tired. When tired, intuitive types fail to notice things, begin to lose things, and get basic facts wrong. A good example is when the intuitive type drives to a meeting in an unfamiliar town, parks the car in a side street while thinking about the meeting, gets out of the car and completely fails to pick up any clues about the location. Cars parked in this way can be very hard to find after the meeting.

For sensing types it is the less preferred function of intuition which lets them down when they are tired. When tired, sensing types fail to see how the pieces fit together, cannot work out what things really mean, and begin to sink under piles of undigested information. A good example is how the sensing type may puzzle for hours over an apparently intractable problem and just cannot get a new angle on it, or see it from a new perspective. Problems tackled in this way can be very hard to resolve.

Given such a fundamental difference between sensing and intuitive types, it is not surprising that they can sometimes easily misunderstand each other. On the one hand, sensing types may experience intuitive types as people who are impractical daydreamers and impossible to pin down to face facts and reality. On the other hand, intuitive types may experience sensing types as people who are far too literalistic, materialistic, unimaginative, and dull. The truth of the matter is that sensing and intuitive types perceive the world in very different ways.

However, once they get to know and to respect each other's individuality, sensing and intuitive types can complement each other's skills and approaches to life. Sensing types can benefit from intuitive types in many ways. For example, intuitive types can:
• help sensing types to develop a vision of future possibilities;
• enable sensing types to approach difficulties with new insights;
• encourage sensing types to manage change positively;
• help sensing types to see and to live with alternatives;
• help sensing types to look at old problems in a new light;
• remind sensing types that future possibilities are worth anticipating and working toward.

Similarly, intuitive types can benefit from sensing types in many ways too. For example, sensing types:
• bring relevant facts to the attention of intuitive types;
• encourage intuitive types to read the instructions on the box and the fine print in the contract;
• inject a dose of realism into the dreams cherished by intuitive types;

- keep records and know where things are when intuitive types are likely to lose touch;
- draw the attention of intuitive types to essential details, facts, and data;
- remind intuitive types that life is for living today.

EXERCISE

Find the pairs of items in the Francis Psychological Type Scales which are listed in Table 6.3. Where you have placed a tick in the box against the response, enter the value 1 in Table 6.3. Where you have left the box blank, enter the value 0. These are the items designed to differentiate between preferences for thinking and for feeling. Now add up the two columns. The higher of the two scores indicates your psychological preference and the difference between the two scores indicates the clarity of your preference between feeling and thinking. If both columns add up to five, then count yourself as preferring feeling. On this occasion do your self-assessment in Chapter 5 and the indicator agree or disagree? What do you learn about yourself from this?

TABLE 6.3 Judging process

thinking		feeling
concern for justice	or	concern for harmony
analytic	or	sympathetic
thinking	or	feeling
tend to be firm	or	tend to be gentle
critical	or	affirming
logical	or	humane
truthful	or	tactful
sceptical	or	trusting
seek for truth	or	seek for peace
fair-minded	or	warm-hearted

Total T score　　　　　　　　**Total F score**

Thinking and feeling

If you are still puzzled about your real preference between thinking and feeling, a very good test is to examine how you react when you are feeling tired. It is your less preferred function which is most likely to let you down.

For thinking types (like the author) it is the less preferred function of feeling which lets them down when they are tired. When tired, thinking types fail to take into account other people's feelings, fail to predict other people's emotional reactions, and can really hurt other people without intending to do so. A good example is how the thinking types may analyse out the issues behind a conflict and then expect the people involved in the conflict to agree with and be helped by the analysis. The analysis may well be true and fair, but nonetheless deeply hurtful and capable of provoking anger.

For feeling types it is the less preferred function of thinking which lets them down when they are tired. When tired, feeling types fail to be able to analyse out what is actually going on in a situation. They get drawn into the situation, and they find it very difficult to stand back and to be objective. They can themselves become quite easily hurt. A good example is how feeling types may try all too hard to empathise with both sides of a quarrel, or with both parties in a conflict. Feeling types may long so much to bring comfort to those who are distressed and to introduce harmony to where there is conflict that they end up being torn apart themselves by the situation they want to resolve.

Given such a fundamental difference between thinking and feeling types, it is not surprising that they can sometimes and so easily misunderstand each other. On the one hand, feeling types may experience thinking types as people who are cold and sometimes even irritatingly condescending. On the other hand, thinking types may experience feeling types as people who are overly emotional and sometimes even sentimental and irrational. The truth of the matter is that feeling and thinking types deal with the world in very different ways.

However, once they get to know and to respect each other's individuality, thinking and feeling types can complement each other's skills and approaches to life. Feeling types can benefit from thinking types in many ways. For example, thinking types can:
• help feeling types to analyse facts and situations;

- support feeling types to face up to people in unpleasant situations;
- help feeling types to find the flaws and hidden traps in human situations;
- help feeling types to stand firm in the face of opposition;
- enable feeling types to think things through with objectivity;
- help feeling types to hold to principles in the face of strong criticism.
  Similarly, thinking types can benefit from feeling types in many ways too. For example, feeling types can:
- help thinking types see how other people feel about things;
- help thinking types to keep an eye on the importance of interpersonal values;
- help thinking types to develop perspectives of empathy and sympathy;
- help thinking types to build up enthusiasm for and personal involvement in things;
- promote recognition among thinking types of the need for harmony and reconciliation;
- value and appreciate thinking types in their own right.

EXERCISE

Find the pairs of items in the Francis Psychological Type Scales which are listed in Table 6.4. Where you have placed a tick in the box against the response, enter the value 1 in Table 6.4. Where you have left the box blank, enter the value 0. These are the items designed to differentiate between preferences for judging and for perceiving. Now add up the two columns. The higher of the two scores indicates your psychological preference and the difference between the two scores indicates the clarity of your preference between judging and perceiving. If both columns add up to five, then count yourself as preferring perceiving. On this occasion do your self-assessment in Chapter 5 and the indicator agree or disagree? What do you learn about yourself from this?

TABLE 6.4 Attitude toward the outer world

judging		perceiving
happy with routine	or	unhappy with routine
structured	or	open-ended
act on decisions	or	act on impulse
like to be in control	or	like to be adaptable
orderly	or	easygoing
organised	or	spontaneous
punctual	or	leisurely
like detailed planning	or	dislike detailed planning
happier with certainty	or	seek for peace
systematic	or	casual
Total J score		**Total P score**

Judging and perceiving

If you are still puzzled about your real preferences between judging and perceiving, a very good test is to examine how you react under pressure or when you are tired. Judging and perceiving types react in very different ways. Once again it is your less preferred function which is most likely to let you down.

For judging types (like the author) it is the less preferred function of perceiving which lets them down when they are tired or under pressure. When tired, judging types become less flexible and more rigid. They are unable to respond to new challenges and panic about their ability to achieve things on time. A good example is when a judging type is asked to make a public presentation at short notice, even about something on which he or she is well skilled. The judging type begins to make lists of what needs to be prepared, despairs that there is insufficient time to get everything organised, and freezes in panic. For the perceiving type, on the other hand, an invitation given at the last minute provides the very pressure needed for a good presentation.

For perceiving types it is the less preferred function of judging which lets them down when they are tired or under pressure. When tired, perceiving types become more difficult to pin down, more elusive when decisions are required, and more reluctant to engage in realistic planning. A good example is when a perceiving type is asked to plan an event months before it is due to take place. Somehow the perceiving type is completely unable to think ahead, to anticipate what is needed, and to make the essential arrangements well in advance. It is not until the last minute that everything begins to fall into place and others are expected to comply. For the judging type, on the other hand, an invitation to plan well in advance provides the very structure and framework needed for a good presentation.

Given such a fundamental difference between judging and perceiving types, it is not surprising that they can sometimes easily misunderstand each other. On the one hand, judging types may experience perceiving types as people who are downright disorganised, messy, and even irresponsible in their approach to life. On the other hand, perceiving types may experience judging types as people who are too demanding, rigid, inflexible and uptight. The truth of the matter is that judging and perceiving types deal with the world in very different ways.

However, once they get to know and to respect each other's individuality, judging and perceiving types can complement each other's skills and attitude toward the world. Perceiving types can benefit from judging types in many ways. For example, judging types can:

- help perceiving types to make decisions;
- provide a framework of structure and routine for perceiving types;
- give perceiving types a sense of time and of the passing of time;
- ensure that necessary jobs really do get done;
- remind perceiving types of schedules and deadlines;
- remind perceiving types that there are some ultimate authorities.

Similarly, judging types can benefit from perceiving types in many ways too. For example, perceiving types can:

- help judging types not to try to settle things too quickly;
- draw to the attention of judging types the variety of different options;
- save judging types from the tyranny of routine;
- help judging types to keep rules and authorities in perspective;
- help judging types to respond to the needs of the moment and to enjoy doing so.

> **EXERCISE**
> In Chapter 5 you formulated an assessment of your own psychological type and now in Chapter 6 you have calculated your scores recorded on the Francis Psychological Type Scales. How easy do you feel it is to measure psychological type?

Reliability

The question of reliability was first raised in Chapter 2. The idea of reliability concerns just how much a psychological test can be relied on to produce the same result on different occasions. If you filled in a psychological type indicator today and again next week, what would be the chances of you coming out with exactly the same type on both occasions?

In this book you have been introduced to the Francis Psychological Type Scales, which is a new test of psychological type, and the real scientific work of establishing its reliability is still underway. Much more, however, is known about an older test, the Myers-Briggs Type Indicator (MBTI). We will, therefore, examine the research literature concerning the reliability of the MBTI.

TABLE 6.5 The sixteen psychological types

ISTJ	ISFJ	INFJ	INTJ
ISTP	ISFP	INFP	INTP
ESTP	ESFP	ENFP	ENTP
ESTJ	ESFJ	ENFJ	ENTJ

The objective of the MBTI, like other type indicators, is primarily to sort individuals into the sixteen discrete type categories as classically displayed in Table 6.5. A number of studies over the years have examined the test-retest of the MBTI by administering the instrument to the same group of people on two different occasions, leaving a clearly defined period of time between the two administrations. Data of this nature have been reported, for example, by Stricker and Ross (1964), Levy, Murphy and Carlson (1972), Howes and Carskadon (1979),

McCarley and Carskadon (1983), Silberman, Freeman and Lester (1992), Johnson (1992), Bents and Wierschke (1996) and Tsuzuki and Matsui (1997).

The proportion of subjects classified with identical categorisations at the retest varies considerably from one study to another. For example, Levy, Murphy and Carlson (1972), in a study among 433 undergraduates, found that after a two month period 53% were assigned the same type on both occasions, while 35% differed on one of the four scales, 10% on two scales, and the remaining 2% on three scales. Howes and Carskadon (1979), in a study among 117 undergraduates, found that after a five week period 49% were assigned the same type on both occasions, while 38% differed on one scale, and the remaining 13% differed on two scales. McCarley and Carskadon (1983) found that after a five week period 47% of their participants retained their specific dichotomous type preferences across all four scales. Silberman, Freeman and Lester (1992) administered the MBTI to 161 dental students before the beginning of their first quarter and again near the end of their fourth year. They found that 24% were assigned the same type on both occasions, while the remaining 76% differed on at least one of the four scales. This study fails to report on the number of scales on which differences occurred. Bents and Wierschke (1996) administered the MBTI to 40 adults twice over a six week period. They found that 68% were assigned the same type on both occasions, while 25% differed on one scale, and the remaining 7% differed on two scales. Tsuzuki and Matsui (1997) administered the MBTI to 88 students twice over a three month period. They found that 33% were assigned the same type on both occasions, while 48% differed on one scale, 16% differed on two scales, and 3% differed on three scales.

Given the difficulty that the MBTI experiences in locating individuals within precisely the same one of the sixteen type categories on two consecutive occasions, we would be wise to treat feedback from the indicator with an appropriate level of caution. The real difficulties occur when our preference between the two oppositing categories is not that strong. Next time we take the test we might well slip across the other side of the dividing line. When preferences are clear and strong, however, readings from the type indicator are much more likely to remain stable over time. In other words, the problem is, say, less to do with grading people as either more or less introvert or extravert, but with knowing precisely where and how to cut a line down the middle, pushing extraverts to one side and introverts to the other side.

When the MBTI is used not to create distinct personality types, but to grade individuals between the four poles of introversion-extraversion, sensing-intuition, thinking-feeling, and judging-perceiving, the reliability statistics are really quite impressive. Data examining the internal consistency reliability, generally in terms of the alpha coefficient (Cronbach, 1951), have been reported, for example, by Stricker and Ross (1963), Tzeng, Ware, Outcalt and Boyer (1985), Cowan (1989), Harvey and Murry (1994), Saggino and Kline (1995) and Tsuzuki and Matsui (1997).

Generally, these studies report internal reliability coefficients in excess of the minimum criteria of 0.7 established by Kline (1993) or of 0.65 established by de Vellis (2003). For example, in four samples of high school students and undergraduates, Stricker and Ross (1963) reported alpha coefficients of .78, .83, .76 and .78 for EI, .77, .74, .75 and .80 for SN, .64, .70, .74 and .71 for TF, and .78, .81, .84 and .81 for JP. According to Harvey (1996), the data on a mixed sample of 1,676 respondents reported by Harvey and Murry (1994) demonstrated alpha coefficients of .84 for EI, .87 for SN, .85 for TF, and .86 for JP. Then, pooling data from three studies generating around 2,400 respondents, Harvey (1996) calculated alpha coefficients of .86 for EI, .87 for SN, .85 for TF, and .87 for JP. In a mixed sample of 1,798 individuals, Saggino and Kline (1995) reported alpha coefficients of .74 for EI, .78 for SN, .67 for TF (male), .56 for TF (female), and .78 for JP. In a sample of 88 students, Tsuzuki and Matsui (1997) reported alpha coefficients of .81 for EI, .78 for SN, .77 for TF, and .81 for JP.

Conclusion

This chapter has examined how type indicators can be employed to help individuals report on their psychological type. At the same time, the chapter has illustrated the difficulties involved in assessing psychological type with precision. Although we need to exercise proper caution when listening to the findings from type indicators, it would be a mistake not to take such evidence seriously alongside our individual perceptions of type. The next chapter will focus attention on further issues raised by type theory.

Further reading

Baron, R (1998), *What Type Am I?: discover who you really are*, New York, Penguin Books.

Carr, S (1997), *Type clarification: finding the fit*, Oxford, Oxford Psychologists Press.

Hedges, P (1993), *Understanding Your Personality: with Myers-Briggs and more*, London, Sheldon Press.

Hirsh, S and Kise, J A G (1998), *Soul Types: finding the spiritual path that is right for you*, New York, Hyperion.

Hirsh, S and Kummerow, J (1989), *Life Types*, New York, Warner Books.

Kroeger, O and Thuesen, J M (1992) *Type Talk at Work*, New York, Delacorte Press.

Myers, I B (2000), *Introduction to Type*, Oxford, Oxford Psychologists Press.

Tieger, P D, Swick, M A and Barron-Tieger, B (1999), *The Art of Speed Reading People*, Boston, Little Brown and Company.

7. DEVELOPING AND CRITIQUING PSYCHOLOGICAL TYPE

Introduction

Chapters 5 and 6 have provided a general introduction to psychological type theory and to the opportunities and problems involved in trying to assess psychological type by means of type indicators. The present chapter builds on these foundations in two ways. First, the component parts of psychological type are examined in greater detail in order to explore the notion of type dynamics. Second, attention is turned to examining the major criticisms raised against type theory both in the secular literature and in the religious literature.

Reflecting on experience

You will now have chosen for yourself four letters to describe your psychological type: either E or I, either S or N, either T or F, either J or P. The middle two letters describe your preferences for the two key psychological processes of perceiving (either S or N) and judging (either T or F). Now think about your own preference pattern for perceiving and for judging when these two are combined (either SF, ST, NF or NT) and ask two questions. Which of the two is your stronger, better developed function? Which of the two do you habitually use in the outer world?

Type dynamics

The two processes concerned with perceiving (sensing and intuition) and judging (thinking and feeling) stand at the heart of Jung's model of psychological type. According to the theory we need to be able to access all four functions (sensing and intuition, thinking and feeling) to be balanced human beings. However, we develop these four functions to different degrees.

Dominant function

According to the theory, one function emerges as our strongest or *dominant* function. It is the development of our dominant function which shapes the person we become and who is recognised by others, once they really get to know us.

The dominant sensing type is seen to be the practical person, who is concerned with making things work. Every church, for example, needs the dominant sensing type to keep an eye on the state of the roof, to make sure that the oil tank is full in winter, to see that the door is unlocked in time for the Sunday morning service, and to check that the hymn numbers are correctly displayed on the board.

The dominant intuitive type is seen to be the ideas person, who is concerned with shaping things for the future. Every church, for example, needs the dominant intuitive type to help shape the mission statement for the future, to keep things moving toward the identified goals, to save the organisation from stagnating, and to come up with imaginative solutions and possibilities when problems and difficulties loom large.

The dominant thinking type is seen to be the systems-orientated person, who is concerned with the integrity and well-being of the organisation. Every church, for example, needs the dominant thinking type to ensure that ministry and mission remain on track with the basic theology of the church, to keep an eye on the principles underpinning practice, to test the truth of the teaching, to maintain the cause of truth, logic and justice, and to be concerned with the theological underpinning of what this church is doing.

The dominant feeling type is seen to be the people-orientated person, who is concerned with caring for individuals. Every church, for example, needs the dominant feeling type to look after the pastoral side of things, to make sure that everyone feels loved and valued, to look after the sick, the lonely and the elderly, and to ensure that harmony and good relationships are everywhere maintained.

Auxiliary functions

According to the theory, the dominant function is supported by a second or auxiliary function. The auxiliary function is always drawn from a different process from that of the dominant function. If the dominant function is S or N, the auxiliary is always T or F; if the dominant function is T or F, the auxiliary is always S or N. This combination leads to eight preference pairs: dominant sensing with auxiliary feeling; dominant sensing with auxiliary thinking; dominant intuition with auxiliary feeling; dominant intuition with auxiliary thinking; dominant thinking with auxiliary sensing; dominant thinking with auxiliary intuition; dominant feeling with auxiliary sensing; and dominant feeling with auxiliary intuition.

EXERCISE
From what you now know about your type preferences for S and N and for T and F, describe what you might understand about the strengths of your dominant and auxiliary functions. Can you guess what is your dominant function?

Inferior function

According to the theory the *inferior* function is the least developed function. It is the opposite of the dominant function. So if your dominant is N, the inferior will be S, and if your dominant is S, the inferior will be N. If your dominant is T, the inferior will be F, and if your dominant is F, the inferior will be T. It is the inferior function which is most likely to let you down when you are tired or working under pressure. It is the inferior function which is most likely to cause problems when people of different type preferences are trying to work together.

For the dominant sensing type, the inferior function is intuition. The practical person who keeps the church tank full of oil, who keeps an eye on the state of the roof and who makes sure that the door is unlocked on time, is also the person who is going to have greatest difficulty in catching a new dream for the church's future. Inferior intuition will dislike change, distrust vision and resist innovation.

For the dominant intuitive type, the inferior function is sensing. The ideas person who tries to keep the local church moving, who wants to save the organisation from stagnation and who suggests ways in which the vision for the future might be shaped, is also the person who is going to have greatest difficulty in facing facts and recognising the very real limitations of the situation. Inferior sensing will fail to notice the cracks in the wall, underestimate the cost of renovation, and refuse to be grounded by reality.

For the dominant thinking type, the inferior function is feeling. The system-orientated person, who is concerned with the integrity and well-being of the organisation, who ensures that the ministry and mission remain on track with the basic theology of the church and who is the champion for truth, logic and justice, is also the person who is most likely to cause the greatest degree of upset and hurt in the church. Inferior feeling will fail to take into account just how individual people will be affected by what is said and by what is done.

For the dominant feeling type, the inferior function is thinking. The people-orientated person, who is concerned with caring for individuals, who looks after the pastoral side of the church, and who makes sure that everyone really feels valued and loved, is also the person who is most likely to lose sight of the core teaching of the church. Inferior thinking will fail to notice when the integrity of the Gospel has been compromised by excessive compassion, or when the pastoral care shown to certain damaged individuals makes the local congregation vulnerable to abuse or harm by those very individuals.

Tertiary function

According to the theory the *tertiary* function is the opposite of the auxiliary function. The tertiary function is less well developed than the auxiliary function, but not so undeveloped as the inferior function.

EXERCISE
From what you now know about your type preferences for S and N and for T and F, describe what you might understand about the weaknesses of your tertiary and inferior functions. Can you guess which is your inferior function?

Type dynamics and orientation

According to the theory, the dominant function is treated differently by extraverts and by introverts. Both use their dominant function in their preferred world. For extraverts the preferred world is the outer world, and consequently extraverts put their dominant function to work in the outer world. For introverts the preferred world is the inner world and consequently introverts put their dominant function to work in the inner world.

The auxiliary function, on the other hand, is employed in the less preferred world. For extraverts the less preferred world is the inner world and it is here in the inner world that extraverts put the auxiliary function to work. For introverts the less preferred world is the outer world and it is here in the outer world that introverts put the auxiliary function to work.

The way in which the dominant and auxiliary functions are employed differently by introverts and by extraverts is crucial to grasping the significance of type dynamics. When you meet an extravert you come face to face with that person's dominant function at work in the outer world. When you meet an introvert, however, you come face to face with that person's auxiliary function in the outer world. You have to wait to get to know the introvert quite well before you begin to recognise that person's real strengths.

I can illustrate this point by drawing on my own personality preference. My dominant function is intuition. As an introvert I employ my dominant function in my inner world. That is where I am imaginative and creative. My auxiliary function is thinking. As an introvert I employ my auxiliary function in the outer world. When people first meet me, what they see is the thinking type. It takes time to get to know me before my real strengths as an intuitive type become properly recognised.

Understanding your type

All the information we need to work out which are our dominant and auxiliary functions is contained in the string of four letters we have selected for ourselves. I will now demonstrate how to read psychological type, again by drawing on my own type profile. I am INTJ. There are four steps to reading these letters.

The first step is to examine the last letter which must be either P or

J. In my case it is J. This tells me that I prefer to use a judging function in the outer world. So I need to examine my judging function next.

The second step, therefore, is to examine my preference between the two judging functions, either T or F. In my case it is T. We now know that I use T in my outer world. When people first meet me, it is likely to be a thinking person whom they see.

The third step is to examine my preference between the two orientations, either E or I. In my case it is I. We now know that as an introvert I use not my dominant function but my auxiliary function in the outer world. Since we already know that I use T in the outer world, we can draw the conclusion that T is my auxiliary function.

The fourth step is to turn attention to the one remaining letter which must be S or N. In my case it is N. We already know that T is my auxiliary function, leaving N to be identified as my dominant function.

In other words INTJ can be described as 'dominant introverted intuition' with 'auxiliary extraverted thinking'.

This process now needs repeating for a second psychological type in order to demonstrate just how the process works. This time I will focus on a colleague, John, my exact opposite in psychological terms. John is ESFP.

The first step is to examine the last letter which must be either P or J. This time it is P. This tells me that John prefers to use a perceiving function in the outer world. So I need to examine John's perceiving function next.

The second step, therefore, is to examine John's preference between the two perceiving functions, either S or N. This time it is S. Now we know that John uses S in the outer world. When people first meet John, it is likely to be a sensing person whom they see.

The third step is to examine John's preference between the two orientations, either E or I. This time it is E. We now know that as an extravert John uses his dominant function in the outside world. Since we already know that John uses S in the outer world, we can draw the conclusion that S is John's dominant function.

The fourth step is to turn attention to the one remaining letter which must be T or F. This time it is F. We already know that S is John's dominant function, leaving F to be identified as John's auxiliary function.

In other words, ESFP can be described as 'dominant extraverted sensing' with 'auxiliary introverted feeling'.

EXERCISE
Now you know how to read type, take your own set of type letters
and work out your dominant and auxiliary functions. Then provide a brief description of how you have followed the four steps
outlined above in order to describe your type.

Criticising type theory

Before turning in Chapters 8, 9 and 10 to three specific areas in which
type theory can be applied within the Christian churches, the second
part of the present chapter turns attention to some of the major criticisms voiced against type theory in both the secular literature and the
religious literature.

From the point of view of the secular literature, in his book, *The
Myers-Briggs Type Indicator: a critical review and practical guide*, Bayne
(1995, pp. 76-93) lists a number of frequently voiced criticisms of type
theory.

Five criticisms

The first criticism noted by Bayne is that type theory is an insult to
individuality. In response Bayne argues that type theory does not try to
capture individuality, but rather provides a broad framework which
helps people move toward appreciating individuality. Type theory
offers four major 'compass points in the wilderness of the psyche'. This
first criticism is, however, a salutary warning against allowing type
theory to degenerate into stereotyping.

The second criticism noted by Bayne is that people behave differently in different situations. People are flexible individuals who have a rich
repertoire of selves from which to choose. Part of being fully human is
the capability to select different identities to project into different situations. Bayne conceptualises this criticism in terms of the wider debate
between two different ways of accounting for human behaviour: the
debate between situation and personality. While recognising that there
is a clear interaction between situation and personality, Bayne argues
that the research evidence for the underlying consistency in human
behaviour across different situations makes it impossible simply to dis-
miss the predictive power of personality theories.

The third criticism noted by Bayne is that the descriptions given in the feedback from some type indicators are too vague and too general. The idea behind this criticism is that the type descriptions are sufficiently general for most people to see themselves in the descriptions given to several (or many) different types. This criticism may in fact misunderstand the nature and purpose of the descriptions given by type indicators. While it is clearly impossible to sum up an individual in a few sentences, the type descriptors can be very useful tools in helping individuals to assess their preferred and habitual ways of functioning. Type descriptors should never be used to tell people their preferred type, but to help them on the slow and crucial path to greater self-insight and self-awareness.

The fourth criticism noted by Bayne is that type descriptors tend to be too positive. The descriptions of the sixteen types provided in the manual to the Myers-Briggs Type Indicator by Myers, McCaulley, Quenk and Hammer (1998), for example, consistently emphasise the strengths of each type, with comparatively little attention placed on the weaknesses. However, the further discussion of type takes good care to enable individuals to examine the opposite of their strengths. In response to this criticism, Bayne draws attention to the important psychological strategy of offering people's strengths before helping them to address their weaknesses.

The fifth criticism noted by Bayne is more technical and suggests that much that is written on type theory misses key aspects of Jung's wider understanding of psychological type. In particular, it is argued by some critics that Jung would want to give greater weight to the role of the unconscious. While this may be so, it has also to be recognised that some aspects of Jung's theory are themselves highly contentious and that it may be a serious error to take a fundamentalist attitude toward Jung's own writings. Currently there is much better empirical support for the model of personality assessment promoted by some of the type indicators than from basic Jungian views.

EXERCISE

Look back over the five criticisms listed above. How damaging do you feel they really are for making use of psychological type theory in the service of faith? Assess each criticism in turn.

Four more criticisms

The sixth criticism noted by Bayne is that type indicators only measure how people answer questionnaires, not how they actually behave in real life. This is the fundamental criticism regarding the validity of pencil and paper tests of personality. The issue has been discussed in the earlier chapter on validity. The mistake, however, is to confuse personality with behaviour. Personality is the underlying stable predisposition which gives rise to behaviour. There are, however, many other intervening factors which sometimes obscure the direct link between personality and behaviour. For example, the introvert who is employed to do an extravert job needs to allow the work context to override the personal preference as much as possible.

The seventh criticism noted by Bayne concerns the confusion caused by preference scores. When individuals are given feedback, say for the Myers-Briggs Type Indicator, they are provided not only with their preferred letters (I or E, S or N, T or F, J or P), but also with the preference scores. The preference scores reflect how consistently the individuals chose items in the questionnaire. A high preference score shows clarity and consistency of choice. A low preference score shows that a number of items were assessed in a way not consistent with the named preference. It is low preference scores which suggest that next time the test is taken a different result may emerge.

The eighth criticism noted by Bayne is that 'the MBTI is unnecessary and just a racket for making money'. This criticism concerns the high costs associated with qualifying to become a Myers-Briggs practitioner in the first instance and then with purchasing the products necessary to function as a practitioner. The publisher would probably offer the defence that psychological tools of this nature are expensive to develop and that it is important that the professional use of such tools should be properly controlled, licensed and policed.

The ninth and final criticism noted by Bayne is that 'type is just like astrology'. There is in fact so little similarity between the two systems that this criticism is hard to sustain. The strengths of psychological type theory are that it is based on empirical observation, and that the profiles offered to individuals are a function of the way in which they have reported their type through the self-completion questionnaire.

At this point it is also worth distinguishing between the notion of psychological type and the Enneagram. Like type indicators the Enneagram is also often applied in association with a self-completion questionnaire. The theory underpinning the Enneagram, however, is not derived from modern psychology, but from Sufi mysticism. Although employed in programmes of Christian spirituality, and often spoken about in the same breath as the Myers-Briggs Type Indicator, the Enneagram belongs to a very different worldview. Criticisms of the Enneagram cannot be uncritically generalised to apply to type theory as well. Introductions to the Enneagram are provided, for example, by Palmer (1995) and Mahon (1998).

EXERCISE

Look back over the four criticisms listed above. How damaging do you feel they really are for making use of psychological type theory in the service of faith? Assess each criticism in turn.

Religious objections

From the point of view of the religious literature, in his booklet *Myers-Briggs: some critical reflections*, Kenneth Leech (1996) drew together a collection of eight essays critiquing psychological type from a range of different perspectives. As a group the different authors are concerned 'about the naive and uncritical devotion exhibited by church groups, including religious communities' to the Myers-Briggs Type Indicator.

In the first essay, Tony Coxon (1996) considers the use of the Myers-Briggs Type Indicator to be one of the 'fads and fashions' of the contemporary church. Commenting as a sociologist Coxon is puzzled by what he sees to be the church's uncritical acceptance of this psychological tool. In response to this question he discusses three main themes. The first theme is that uncritical acceptance of the Myers-Briggs Type Indicator is consistent with the ways in which other psychological theories have been embraced uncritically by the church, and he points specifically to 'clinical theology' as promoted by Frank Lake (1996). James Fowler's (1981) 'faith development' theory could well come into the same category. The second theme is that the apparent certainty offered by psychological theories is particularly attractive within churches which have lost confidence in the theological understanding of their role. The third theme is that the 'special knowledge' held by Myers-Briggs Type Indicator practitioners provides a source of power and authority. It is a kind of 'revealed knowledge' so powerful in religious gnostic traditions.

In the second essay, Heather Ward (1996) is concerned that tools like the Myers-Briggs Type Indicator try to reduce spirituality to a branch of psychology rather than recognising spirituality as a branch of theology. Historically, she argues, 'spiritualities were intent upon an exploration into God rather than an exploration of ourselves'. She maintains that contemporary spiritualities are in danger of replacing 'theology and ontology with psychology, and spirit with personality'. This has shifted the primary focus away from God and onto ourselves.

Heather Ward's second point is that spirituality based on psychological models runs the risk of emphasising autonomy and self-fulfilment at the expense of relationships and duty. Such emphasis, she argues, 'colludes with a life-view which values experience as a form of possession and which tends to view the self as a commodity to be re-modelled and enhanced'.

In the third essay, Richard Woods (1996) takes quite a sympathetic view of the Myers-Briggs Type Indicator, but remains anxious about the uncritical use of the instrument in spiritual direction. He argues that 'psychological type at most provides a hypothesis regarding some of the ways in which people might develop spirituality. When used for guidance, it is only a map, not the territory, and emphatically not the journey itself.' Sight should never be lost of 'the distinct and individual uniqueness of the person and her developmental process'. According to Woods, an uncritical, inappropriate application of psychological type theory may not only fail to illuminate the inner life, 'but also obscure and even disfigure it by substituting a quick and partial profile for the long, necessarily gradual and often gruelling process of self-discovery (and divine revelation)'.

In the fourth essay, John Davies (1996) writes as a psychologist who is totally unconvinced by the science of psychological measurement. He claims 'the utmost scepticism concerning claims made that particular psychometric tests measure in any real sense mental entities'. Such fundamental scepticism clearly precludes Davies from seeing any value in type theory for the church.

In the fifth essay, Dick Joyce (1996) voices a dislike for employing psychological tests 'to select candidates for the ministry', or for matching clergy to specific parishes. In part he is not convinced that the instruments are capable of being used effectively in such ways.

In the sixth essay, Anthony Egan (1996) focuses on the problem of determinism. He detects in some of the literature, connected both with psychological type in general and with psychological type and spirituality in particular, a form of naive determinism. It is this that he rejects, since it militates against the richness of human potential. Egan also raises the danger of type theory placing excessive emphasis on the importance of 'me', with consequent cost to appreciating the value of the family and the value of the wider society.

In the seventh essay, John Reader (1996) rehearses two reasons why the church should exercise caution about using psychological type theory. The first reason is based on doubts about the reliability of the measurements provided by type indicators. He writes as follows (p. 32).

> What concerns me are the claims that are being made for these techniques and the way they are being employed by the institutional church. Can Myers-Briggs really tell us what approach to spirituality is appropriate to us as individuals? Should it be used as a way of assessing potential ordinands? If the method is not as reliable as some suggest are we not in danger of labelling, stereotyping and ultimately trying to control other people?

The second reason is based on anxieties about the ways in which type theory can be misrepresented. He writes as follows (p. 33).

> Myers-Briggs, if used within its limitations, can contribute to the developing critical consciousness of the individual by encouraging reflection upon questions of identity. But, when it is employed as a technique for providing secure answers and closing down options it can only hamper that process.

In the eighth essay, Andy Delmerge (1996) argues that psychological type theory attempts to answer, through a pencil and paper test, the ultimate question about the nature of being which has perplexed philosophers from the time of 'the ancient Greeks'. He then criticises the 'Myers-Briggs personality test' in particular for failing to answer this ultimate question. He concludes his essay as follows (p. 38).

> In conclusion we have seen that MBTI is an unsuccessful attempt at the question of Being, offering us inadequate, incorrect and crude answers. We should therefore treat it with an enormous amount of caution because it singularly fails to do justice either to our being or to Being in general. We are still left with a great deal of work before we can answer the question of Being. MBTI has shown us some insufficient methods and answers; perhaps the interest and devotion it has engendered can be used positively to spur us on to face the

question in a rather more careful and truthful way. We must reject easy answers, admitting that we are a people who no longer understand our being and are in perplexity and darkness much of the time.

EXERCISE
Look back over the summaries of the eight essays collected by Kenneth Leech, critiquing the use of psychological type theory within the churches. How damaging do you feel they really are for making use of psychological type theory in the service of faith? Assess the contribution of each author in turn.

Responding to criticism

The present author went away from Leech's collection of essays feeling disappointed rather than bruised. All eight authors clearly disliked the application of type theory to the fields of ministry, mission and spirituality, but their dislike was supported more by rhetoric than by sustained argument. Overall they were tending to misrepresent and to misinterpret the claims made for the application of type theory within church-related fields. Three main threads run through the criticisms.

The first thread maintains that psychological type theory can be misused by churches. This is clearly true and this is why it is important that those who wish to apply the insights of psychological type theory to church-related fields need to be properly informed and properly equipped from both psychological and theological perspectives. Awareness concerning the dangers of misuse, however, can lead to better practice, and not simply to prejudiced rejection.

The second thread maintains that reliance on psychological type theory misrepresents Christian spirituality by directing attention toward psychology and away from theology. Such an accusation certainly misunderstands the way in which approaches like the one adopted by the present book advocate the application of type theory to spirituality. Such an accusation also drives an inappropriate wedge between the activities of psychology and theology and ignores the kinds of argument advanced by the present book for the proper application of psychological methods and theories within the discipline of theology itself.

The third thread maintains that human personality is itself too complex to be assessed by psychometric tests and that such tests degrade and undervalue the uniqueness of each individual. Such an accusation dismisses the enterprise of modern psychology, assumes that creation itself is random, and questions the fundamental principle of seeking scientifically discernable patterns underpinning the created universe. Such challenges may be too ambitious to sustain.

Conclusion

This chapter has developed and critiqued the idea of psychological type. You should now be in a better position to know how to read your own psychological type preferences and to understand the psychological type preferences of other people. You should also be in a better position to evaluate the criticisms raised against type theory and to be aware of the pitfalls in using type theory. Against this background, it is the aim of the remaining three chapters to set type theory to work in three specific faith-related areas.

Further reading

Bayne, R (1995), *The Myers-Briggs Type Indicator: a critical review and practical guide*, London, Chapman and Hall.

Carr, S (1997), *Type clarification: finding the fit*, Oxford, Oxford Psychologists Press.

Dwyer, M T (1995), *No Light without Shadow: an exploration of personality types*, Thornbury, Victoria, Desbooks.

Myers, I B, McCaulley, M H, Quenk, N L and Hammer, A L (1998), *Manual: a guide to the development and use of the Myers-Briggs Type Indicator*, Palo Alto, California, Consulting Psychologists Press.

Myers, K D and Kirby, L K (2000), *Introduction to Type Dynamics and Development*, Oxford, Oxford Psychologists Press.

Quenk, N L (2002), *Was That Really Me?: how everyday stress brings out our hidden personality*, Palo Alto, California, Davies-Black.

Spoto, A (1989), *Jung's Typology in Perspective*, Boston, Massachusetts, Sigo Press.

Thomson, L (1998), *Personality Type: an owner's manual*, Boston, Massachusetts, Shambhala.

8. MINISTRY STYLE AND PSYCHOLOGICAL TYPE

Introduction

Psychological type theory suggests that psychological type preferences may exert a significant influence both on the type of career people choose for themselves and on the ways in which they carry out their work in the career which they have chosen.

Reflecting on experience
Think of some of the people you know in relation to the job they have chosen to do. Can you spot any connection between psychological type preferences and certain careers? For example, to what kind of jobs do you imagine extraverts would gravitate, and to what kind of jobs would introverts gravitate?

Accountants

Two professions which have attracted quite a lot of research from the perspective of psychological type theory are accountants and teachers. I propose to look at what is known about these two professions in turn before examining what is known about the clergy.

A number of studies have examined the psychological type of accountants in the United States of America, including Jacoby (1981), Descouzis (1989) and Satava (1996). Such studies have drawn attention to preferences for introversion, for sensing, for thinking, and for judging among accountants. Overall the most prevalent type was often ISTJ.

In many ways ISTJ seems the ideal sort of person to work in

accounting. Introversion predisposes people to work well alone for long periods. Sensing predisposes people to care about facts and details. Thinking predisposes people to seek out the truth and to fight for objective clarity. Judging predisposes people to seek order and organisation in the outer world. In her *Introduction to Type*, Myers (1998, p. 7) profiles the ISTJ in the following terms:

> Serious, quiet, earn success by concentration and thoroughness. Practical, orderly, matter-of-fact, logical, realistic and dependable. See to it that everything is well organised. Take responsibility. Make up their own minds about what should be accomplished and work toward it steadily, regardless of protests or distractions.

EXERCISE

Reflecting on your own psychological type, how would you feel working as an accountant? Set out how your own psychological preferences fit or fail to fit the way you understand that job.

Teachers

A number of studies have examined the psychological type of elementary school teachers in the United States of America, including Schurr, Henriksen, Moor and Wittig (1993), Sears, Kennedy and Kaye (1997) and Reid (1999). More recently Francis (2004c) has examined the psychological type of 183 female trainee primary school teachers in the United Kingdom. Francis' study demonstrated that, as a group, female primary school teachers displayed clear preferences for extraversion over introversion, for sensing over intuition, for feeling over thinking, and for judging over perceiving. These preferences were quite marked: 67% were extraverts, compared with 33% introverts; 72% were sensing types, compared with 28% intuitive types; 79% were feeling types, compared with 21% thinking types; 63% were judging types, compared with 37% perceiving types. Overall the most prevalent type was ESFJ which described one in every four (25%) of all the female primary school teachers.

In many ways ESFJ seems the ideal sort of person to work in the kind of primary schools which flourish in the United Kingdom. In

Introduction to Type, Myers (1998, p. 7) profiles the ESFJ in the following terms:

> Warm-hearted, talkative, popular, conscientious, born co-operators, active committee members. Need harmony and may be good at creating it. Always doing something nice for someone. Work best with encouragement and praise. Main interest is in things that directly and visibly affect people's lives.

Moreover, since they are in such a clear majority, teachers with preference for extraversion, sensing, feeling and judging can shape the overall expectations of the primary school culture. This will be good for some pupils, but less good for others.

The preference for extraversion may lead to the normative primary classroom favouring an extravert culture. In this extravert culture, a variety of activities will be encouraged. For example, children will be encouraged to talk about what they are doing, thinking and feeling. A level of background noise and social interaction will be assumed as good practice. Children will not be expected to work in silence. Introverted pupils, however, who long for the space to be, for the peace to think, and for an escape from social interaction, could be the potential losers.

The preference for sensing may lead to the normative primary classroom favouring a sensing culture. In this sensing culture, a love for the conventional will be fostered. A lot of attention will be given to the environment, which will tend to be neat and tidy. Lessons will be planned in advance and the criteria of the National Curriculum clearly met. Intuitive pupils, however, who fail to be contained within the carefully constructed sensing environment and whose individuality frustrates the teacher's quest for conformity, could be the potential losers.

The preference for feeling may lead to the normative primary classroom favouring a feeling culture. In this feeling culture, the individuality and individual needs of each child count, at least as far as the teacher perceives their needs. The teacher will take time to relate to each child as an individual human being and to show an interest in the opportunities and constraints afforded by the child's home background. Time will be taken to settle individual children to the tasks in hand. Pupils who prefer thinking, however, whose incisive logic and pursuit of truth and justice may be rejected as insensitive or inappropriate by the feeling teacher, could be the potential losers.

The preference for judging may lead to the normative primary classroom favouring a judging culture. In this judging culture, the school day is carefully planned and well organised from the beginning to the end. The week will be divided into a recognised and recurring pattern. Every Monday follows the same routine. The days will be divided into clear lesson slots. Everyone will know when mathematics will be over and when physical education will begin. Books will be clearly classified and well organised on the class library shelves, and the children's desks or tables will remain in fixed locations. The potential losers, however, could be the perceiving pupils who become so absorbed in the interest of the moment that they habitually arrive late for class or who fail to notice that the transition has taken place from silent reading to classroom mathematics.

EXERCISE
Reflecting on your own psychological type, how would you feel working as a primary school teacher? Set out how your own psychological preferences fit or fail to fit the way you understand that job.

Implications for teachers

Francis (2004c) draws out one further implication from his study of primary school teachers and that concerns the plight of individual teachers who do not fit the dominant mould. He argues that in a culture shaped and dominated by ESFJ preferences, the INFP teacher may experience particular difficulty. The INFP is likely to be attracted to the teaching profession because of the desire to exercise the feeling function in this caring way. The INFP teacher, however, is likely to experience difficulty in having her preference for introversion valued in a predominantly extravert culture. Pupils conditioned to respond to extravert teachers may find her quieter approach to be strange and unfamiliar. The INFP teacher is likely to experience her preference for intuition largely rejected in a predominantly sensing culture. Fellow teachers conditioned to expect sensing-type contributions to staff meetings will find her unpredictable and unquenchable thirst for proposing new, untried, and unproven strategies disconcerting and threatening. The INFP teacher is likely to experience her preference for perceiving to be largely misunderstood in a predominantly judging culture. Pupils conditioned to expect a highly structured environment may find her commitment to openness and flexibility disorienting. Fellow teachers conditioned to find judging-type conditions in the classroom may misunderstand and misrepresent her commitment to a perceiving-type environment as indicative of incompetence, mismanagement and irresponsibility.

Although these difficulties would also confront the INTP within the primary school environment, the implications may be more serious and more profound for the INFP teacher. Like all feeling-types, the INFP needs to feel appreciated and valued. She is, therefore, less able than her INTP colleague to set an objective distance between herself and the reaction she receives from her teaching colleagues.

EXERCISE

Reflecting on what you now know about accountants and primary school teachers, draw up a psychological type profile for a minister of religion, a priest, or a vicar. What sort of psychological characteristics are likely to be required in that job: introversion or extraversion, sensing or intuition, thinking or feeling, judging or perceiving?

Ministry styles

One of the people who has given considerable thought to the ways in which psychological type relate to ministry is Dr John Payne. Dr Payne is an Anglican priest who has also trained in psychology and counselling. His research on the ways in which different clergy understand and express their ministry has led to the development of the Payne Index of Ministry Styles (PIMS), described fully by Francis and Payne (2002).

In this analysis Payne recognises that there is a proper place in ministry for both introverts and extraverts, for both sensing and intuitive types, for both thinking and feeling types, and for both judging and perceiving types. The point is, however, that different psychological types may well choose to express their preferred ministry styles in different ways. As a consequence they may fit some ministry contexts better than others.

Extraversion or introversion

Extraverts and introverts may display very different ministry styles and very different priorities in their ministry. At heart, in Jung's theory, the distinction between introversion and extraversion is concerned with energy sources. The extravert draws energy from the outer world of people and things, while the introvert draws energy from the inner world of ideas and solitude.

Projecting Jung's notion of extraversion onto ministry styles, Payne calculates that extravert clergy would be energised: by visiting groups of people; by going out in the parish and visiting people in their homes; by preaching to a large congregation (and interacting with the people afterwards); by meeting new people in the church (and talking with them); by leading large group meetings; by leading worship with large congregations (and knowing the people); and by being seen out and about in the parish.

Projecting Jung's notion of introversion onto ministry styles, Payne draws up a very different profile. He calculates that introvert clergy would be energised: by spending time alone in prayer; by conducting worship with small groups (and doing so without feeling the need to get to know the individuals well); by giving time to prepare sermons (working alone); by reading about a theological topic in depth; by taking time to read and write in their study; by engaging in a contemplative style of prayer (in solitude); and by giving time to pray for people.

Here are two very different approaches to ministry. The problems come when clergy are expected to operate for too long outside their own preferred style. Introvert ministers who feel that they are expected to spend all their time with people may lose energy and begin to experience burnout. Extravert ministers who find themselves ministering to small churches with little opportunity for meeting and working alongside other people may lose energy and begin to experience burnout.

There is a place for both an extravert ministry style and for an introvert ministry style. The difficulties arise when the needs and the expectations of the church come into conflict with the ministry strengths of the pastor.

Sensing or intuition

Sensing and intuitive types may display very different ministry styles and very different priorities in their ministry. At heart, in Jung's theory, the distinction between sensing and intuition is concerned with the way in which the world is perceived. The sensing type lives in the present and is very aware of current realities. The intuitive type lives more in the future and is very aware of new possibilities.

Projecting Jung's notion of sensing onto ministry styles, Payne calculates that sensing clergy would like to concentrate on the tasks that need to be done in the parish. They would rather be doing practical things in the parish than planning future possibilities. They would take an interest in the church building and ensure that things are kept in good order. They would enjoy being involved in the fine detail of maintaining the church. They would welcome giving a hand in practical matters like painting and decorating the church hall. They would see that keeping detailed accounts is an important part of their ministry.

Projecting Jung's notion of intuition onto ministry styles, Payne draws up a very different profile. He calculates that intuitive clergy would like to think up new ways of doing things in their parish. They would like to shape a new vision for the future of their church. They would enjoy discovering the Gospel truth afresh in their own generation. They would like to question religious tradition whenever they can. They would like to find solutions to new problems and new solutions to old problems. They would enjoy raising questions of faith which others find difficult to answer. They would like to leave people with questions (rather than with answers) when they are preaching sermons.

Here are two very different approaches to ministry. The problems come when clergy are expected to operate for too long outside their own preferred style. Sensing ministers who are in charge of a church which desperately requires a new vision for the future may become very disillusioned by their inability to see a way through the current difficulties. Intuitive ministers who are in charge of a church well settled into its tradition may become very frustrated by their inability to change things and to experiment with new ideas.

There is a place for both a sensing ministry style and for an intuitive ministry style. The difficulties arise when the needs and expectations of the church come into conflict with the ministry strengths of the pastor.

Thinking or feeling

Thinking and feeling types may display very different ministry styles and very different priorities in their ministry. At least, in Jung's theory, the distinction between thinking and feeling is concerned with the way in which information is evaluated and decisions are made. The thinking type lives in the world of the head and is concerned with objectivity, logic and truth. The feeling type lives in the world of the heart and is concerned with subjectivity, human relationships, harmony and peace.

Projecting Jung's notion of thinking onto ministry styles, Payne calculated that thinking clergy would operate their ministry by trying to think through the logical consequences of actions. They would find it helpful to analyse things in a logical manner. They would want to be objective in pastoral crises. They would find it rewarding to settle disputes with parishioners objectively. Above all they would want to be fair and just in dealing with people. They would not find it difficult to take tough decisions in the parish. Overall in their ministry they would rather be effective than liked.

Projecting Jung's notion of feeling onto ministry styles, Payne draws up a very different profile. He calculates that feeling clergy would like to operate their ministry by trying to create a harmonious parish atmosphere. They would like to consider the needs of parishioners above all else. They would say that they find it helpful to deal sensitively with people in the parish. They would like being involved with parishioners and with their problems. Indeed, they would find dealing with the emotional problems of parishioners most rewarding. They would enjoy being in fellowship with others and need the support of knowing that relationships were in good order in the church. Above all they would be responding to God in acts of compassion.

Here are two very different approaches to ministry. The problems come when clergy are expected to operate for too long outside their own preferred style. Thinking clergy are concerned with getting the system of the local church running smoothly. They can find it most debilitating when problems with human relationships and feelings get in the way of the system. Feeling clergy are concerned with getting the relationships right within the local church. They can find it most debilitating when problems with malfunctioning systems distract them from the things that really matter.

There is a place for both a thinking ministry style and for a feeling ministry style. The difficulties arise when the needs and expectations of the church come into conflict with the ministry strengths of the pastor.

Judging and perceiving

Judging and perceiving types may display very different ministry styles and very different priorities in their ministry. At heart, the distinction between judging and perceiving is concerned with the way in which the outer world is approached. The judging type wants the outer world to be well organised, planned and disciplined. The perceiving type wants the outer world to remain open, flexible and spontaneous.

Projecting the notion of judging onto ministry styles, Payne calculates that judging clergy would like to plan things down to the last detail in their parish work. They would argue that good leadership involves good planning in church life. They would try to run their parish according to a strict schedule. They would like services to be well planned and well thought out in advance. They would maintain that any changes in the parish should be carefully thought through and planned. They would want to see that things are kept in order in the church. They would draw up lists of things that need to be done each day in the parish and feel frustrated if other things intervene and prevent the list being carried out.

Projecting the notion of perceiving onto ministry styles, Payne calculates that perceiving clergy would look forward to and enjoy the unpredictability of pastoral ministry. Freedom to be flexible would be an important aspect of ministry for them. Indeed, they would positively enjoy having their routine disturbed. They would like to be flexible in worship and not always tied to time and to order. They would enjoy being spontaneous in services. They would enjoy having variety and unplanned stimulation in their ministry. They would enjoy new and unexpected experiences in their ministry.

Here are two very different approaches to ministry. The problems come when clergy are expected to operate for too long outside their own preferred style. Judging clergy are concerned with running a well-planned church. They can find it most debilitating when people who were planned to read lessons or to carry through administration do not live by the same commitment to plans and to advanced organisation. Perceiving clergy are concerned with being able to respond to new ideas and to reflect changes in the world around them. They can find it most debilitating when the organist wants the hymns a week in advance and the lesson reader will not change the reading at the last minute.

There is a place for both a judging ministry style and for a perceiving ministry style. The difficulties arise when the needs and expectations of the church come into conflict with the ministry strengths of the pastor.

EXERCISE

Reflecting on your own psychological type, how would you see your own preferred ministry style? What would be your strengths and weaknesses in ministry?

Knowing your clergy

A number of studies have reported on the psychological type preferences of religious professionals in the United States of America. For example, in their *Atlas of Type Tables*, Macdaid, McCaulley and Kainz (1986) reported that in a sample of 1,298 Roman Catholic priests, the predominant types were ISFJ (18%), ESFJ (14%), ENFJ (11%), and ENTP (11%). In a sample of 1,554 Protestant ministers, the predominant types were ENFJ (16%), ENFP (14%), and ESFJ (13%).

In their book, *Personality Type and Religious Leadership*, Oswald and Kroeger (1988) reported that in a sample of 1,319 clergy from a wide range of denominations (including Presbyterian, Episcopal, Lutheran, United Church of Christ, Roman Catholic, Disciples of Christ, American Baptist, Southern Baptist, United Methodist, Swedenborgians, Mennonites), the predominant types were ENFJ (16%), ESFJ (12%), and ENFP (12%). In a second sample of 254 Presbyterian clergy, Oswald and Kroeger (1988) found the same pattern: ENFJ (15%), ESFJ (12%), and ENFP (11%).

The first large scale attempt to examine the psychological type preferences of clergy in the United Kingdom was reported by Francis, Payne and Jones (2001). Over a period of eight years a total of 427 male clergy in the Church in Wales completed the Myers-Briggs Type Indicator, either through participation in a ministry training course or in response to a postal survey. The total number of male stipendiary clergy under the age of retirement in the Church in Wales in 1999 was 610. Of the total participants in the survey, 13% were in their twenties, 20% in their thirties, 34% in their forties, 25% in their fifties, and 8% in their sixties.

The strength of the study is that it is able to provide good insight into clergymen in the Church in Wales. The limitation is that generalisations cannot be made to include other denominational groups.

The study by Francis, Payne and Jones (2001) demonstrated that, as a group, male Church in Wales clergy displayed clear preferences for introversion over extraversion, for sensing over intuition, for feeling over thinking, and for judging over perceiving. These preferences were often quite marked: 59% were introverts, compared with 41% extraverts; 57% were sensing types, compared with 43% intuitive types; 69% were feeling types, compared with 31% thinking types; 68% were judging types, compared with 32% perceiving types. Overall the most prevalent type was ISFJ, which described one in every five (20%) of the male Church in Wales clergy.

In many ways ISFJ seems the ideal sort of person to provide the backbone of pastoral ministry and pastoral care. In *Introducing Type*, Myers (1998, p. 7) profiles ISFJ in the following terms.

> Quiet, friendly, responsible and conscientious. Work devotedly to meet their obligations. Lend stability to any project or group. Thorough, painstaking, accurate. Their interests are usually not technical. Can be patient with necessary details. Loyal, considerate, perceptive, concerned with how other people feel.

Understanding your clergy

A Church shaped by preferences for introversion, sensing, feeling and judging will have many strengths. It is important, however, also to be aware of the limitations of such a profile. Francis, Payne and Jones (2001, p. 22) conclude their study of the psychological preferences of male clergy in the Church in Wales with the following analysis. Introverts may bring many strengths to ministry, including the ability to work by themselves on tasks, to invest time in reading and in preparation, to welcome one-to-one encounters in counselling and in spiritual direction, to develop an inward life of prayer and spirituality. On the other hand, introverts may be drained by many of the social expectations of ministry, working with large groups of people, remembering names, visiting strangers and assuming a high profile in the local congregation and in the wider local community.

Sensing types may bring many strengths to ministry, including a fine awareness of the environment in which they serve and of the church in which they lead worship, a concern for the detail within the services they conduct and for the facts on which judgements and choices are made. On the other hand, sensing types may find it more difficult to formulate a vision for their church's future, to welcome change and experimentation in liturgy, or to see new and imaginative solutions to old problems.

Feeling types may bring many strengths to ministry, including the desire to affiliate with others, the gifts of empathy and sympathy, a commitment to harmony, a deep understanding of people and a respect for inter-personal values. On the other hand, feeling types may find it more difficult to take tough decisions which affect other people's lives, to chair troublesome meetings, to be assertive on points of truth and justice, and to put other people in their place.

Judging types may bring many strengths to ministry, including the ability to organise their own lives, to organise the life of their parishes, to arrange services and events well in advance, to keep on top of administration and to manage local affairs. On the other hand, judging types may become too inflexible and restricted by their own strategies, plans and routines, too unwilling or unable to abandon their plans in order to respond to unexpected crises, emergencies or opportunities, and too bound to the present structure to embrace new ideas and possibilities.

A Church which has developed this kind of profile may find it difficult to integrate clergy who take a very different approach to ministry. In particular, clergy with preferences for intuition and for thinking may find ministry within such a Church very frustrating. They may complain about a lack of vision, about a resistance to change, and about a fundamental failure to take tough management decisions.

Some clergy with preferences for intuition and for thinking may choose to remain in the Church in Wales, but increasingly distance themselves from diocesan and provincial policies. Some may choose to cross the border in order to try ministry in England. Others may choose to seek secular employment or sector ministries.

A wider view

Following on from the pioneering study by Francis, Payne and Jones (2001) among Church in Wales clergy, a series of other studies have turned attention to other denominational groups. The main finding from these studies is that male Evangelical clergy are much more likely to prefer thinking than is the case among Church in Wales clergymen. For example, in a study of 278 male Bible College students, Francis, Penson and Jones (2001) found that the most prevalent type was ISTJ (15%). In a study of 164 male church leaders attending Spring Harvest, Craig, Francis and Robbins (2004) found that the most prevalent type was ISTJ (30%). In a study of 81 male Evangelical seminarians Francis, Craig and Butler (2004) also found that the most prevalent type was ISTJ (19%). It seems to be the case that Evangelical churches may attract a more toughminded ministry style.

EXERCISE
Reflecting on what is now known about the psychological profile of clergy, how would you envisage such information could best be used by the churches?

Applying type theory

There are three main ways in which type theory could be of real practical benefit in the development of ministry.

First, type theory can be very beneficial to individual clergy themselves. Recognising how psychological type preferences shape different strengths in ministry should help clergy to identify and to value their own God-given strengths rather than to strive after a form of ministry which is just outside their grasp. For example, introvert ministers need to value their introverted ministry style and not see themselves as failed extraverts.

Second, type theory can help to predict areas of weakness in ministry and to alert clergy to the pitfalls of ministry burnout. Long periods of trying to operate in less preferred ministry styles may lead to exhaustion and to psychological distress. For example, extravert ministers who try to work in relative isolation may find their energy resources too quickly depleted.

Third, type theory can help church leaders, including bishops, to locate clergy in pastoral charges where their strengths in ministry can be deployed to best effect. For example, a failing church which requires a new vision and tough management is unlikely to be best served by an ISFJ leader. A strong traditional church which requires consistent pastoral care and stable nurture is unlikely to be best served by an ENTP leader.

Conclusion

This chapter has examined the implications of psychological type theory for church leadership and ministry style. It has argued that different psychological type preferences lead to different ministry styles and to different strengths and weaknesses in ministry. While no one psychological type preference is clearly the best fit for ministry, different type preferences are likely to be better for different churches.

Further reading

Butler, A (1999), *Personality and Communicating the Gospel*, Cambridge, Grove Books.

Fowke, R (1997), *Finding Your Prayer Personality*, Nashville, Abingdon, Tennessee.

Goldsmith, M (1994), *Knowing Me, Knowing God*, London, Triangle.

Hirsh, S and Kise, J A G (1997), *Looking at Type and Spirituality*, Gainsville, Florida, Centre for Application of Psychological Type.

Keating, C J (1987), *Who We Are is How We Pray*, Mystic, Connecticut, Twenty-Third Publications.

Osborn, L and Osborn, D (1991), *God's Diverse People*, London, Daybreak.

Oswald, R M and Kroeger, O (1988), *Personality Type and Religious Leadership*, Washington, DC, Alban Institute.

Williams, I (1987), *Prayer and My Personality*, Bramcote, Grove Books.

9. CONGREGATIONAL STYLE AND PSYCHOLOGICAL TYPE

Introduction

The previous chapter has examined the implications of psychological type theory for understanding church leaders and ministry styles. The present chapter now turns attention to church congregations and examines the implications of psychological type theory for understanding how congregations function and for interpreting recognisable differences between one congregation and another.

Reflecting on experience

Consider a congregation which you know well. As a group of people, does this congregation seem to have an overall set of psychological type preferences? Does the congregation seem to you to be predominantly introvert or extravert, predominantly sensing or intuitive, predominantly thinking or feeling, predominantly judging or perceiving?

Churchgoers or church leavers

In their study of church leavers, *Gone but not Forgotten*, Philip Richter and Leslie J Francis (1998) distinguish between eight main causes for people leaving church. One of these eight causes they style 'believing but not belonging'. They identified a number of people who left their church congregation, not because they were experiencing fundamental problems with their religious faith, but rather because they had a growing sense of not fitting in or of not belonging to the congregation of which they were part.

Of course, there are many reasons why individuals may feel that they do not fit into their local congregation. Some may feel that the congregation does not really accommodate their own age group. For example, the young parent with two boisterous toddlers may feel out of place in a congregation largely comprising retired people who prefer a quiet and uninterrupted service. Some may feel that the congregation does not really accommodate their own family status. For example, the single person may feel very isolated in the congregation which is totally centred around 'family worship', and the expectation that everyone lives within a stable relationship. Some may feel that the congregation does not really accommodate their theological position. For example, individuals who are exploring an open quest-orientated style of faith may feel inadequate or unaffirmed by a group of people who are overly certain in their own religious convictions.

Alongside reasons concerned with age, family status and faith style, there are other causes underpinning the feeling of not really belonging which may have more to do with the psychological profile of the congregation and of the leadership style. Richter and Francis (1998, p. 129) were alerted to this possibility when they began to analyse some of the points made by their interviewees. For example, Elsie Brooks, a Methodist minister, described the two very different churches of which she had oversight in the following terms.

> One was a large town-centre church with a membership of over two hundred. The other was in a 'village' location and had less than one hundred members. The first church alienated some people because they perceived it as 'too big and impersonal'. The 'family atmosphere' of the second church alienated others because it was 'a bit too close and claustrophobic' and did not appear to offer them 'freedom to be themselves'.

Sarah Johnson described how, after moving house, she and her husband tried to establish themselves in two very different types of churches. The first church they tried frightened them off because it was not friendly enough. The second church they tried frightened them off because it was too friendly. Here the welcome was very personal, but also very stifling. According to Richter and Francis (1998, p. 129), Sarah summed up her reaction as follows.

> We were welcomed with open arms, but welcomed too much, in the fact that in the service we were actually welcomed by name, and made to stand up, and it was, 'Hi, Sarah and the children are here today and the husband Trevor's not with them because he had to go

to work today, but hopefully we'll see him next week?' It was like, 'Oh, my goodness, I can't cope with this, I need the group to open up and swallow me.'

EXERCISE
Draw up the psychological profile of the congregation in which you would feel most at home. Is this congregation predominantly introvert or extravert, predominantly sensing or intuitive, predominantly thinking or feeling, predominantly judging or perceiving? How does this relate to your own psychological profile?

Discovering congregational type preferences

In spite of the potential usefulness and benefits of knowing more about the psychological type profile of church congregations, comparatively little research has been invested in this area of practical theology. A start was made in the United States of America by a study undertaken by Gerhardt (1983). This involved a small sample of 83 adult Unitarian Universalists. Among this sample the data revealed preferences for introversion (59%) over extraversion (41%), for intuition (78%) over sensing (22%), and for judging (67%) over perceiving (33%). The balance was close between thinking (52%) and feeling (48%). In other words, the predominant type profiles were INFJ and INTJ. This profile is consistent with the image of Unitarian Universalists as an open, liberal group which welcomes the critique of the standard orthodox doctrines of Christianity. Here is a style of congregation in which extraverts and sensing types might feel less immediately at home.

A second study in the United States of America was reported by Rehak (1998), this time among a sample of 76 Evangelical Lutherans. Among this sample the data revealed preferences for introversion (68%) over extraversion (32%) and for feeling (74%) over thinking (26%). Even balances were found between sensing (50%) and intuition (50%) and between judging (51%) and perceiving (49%). In other words, the predominant type profiles were ISFJ, INFJ, ISFP and INFP. Here is a style of congregation in which extraverts and thinking types might feel less immediately at home.

Research in Canada is reported by Delis-Bulhoes (1990) and by Ross (1995). Delis-Bulhoes studied Francophone Roman Catholics and

Evangelical Protestants, with samples of 48 Catholics and 154 Protestants. Among the Protestants, the data revealed preferences for introversion (71%) over extraversion (29%), for sensing (88%) over intuition (12%), for thinking (62%) over feeling (38%), and for judging (62%) over perceiving (38%). Among the Catholics, the data revealed preferences for introversion (65%) over extraversion (35%), for sensing (72%) over intuition (28%), for feeling (57%) over thinking (43%), and for judging (67%) over perceiving (33%). Ross (1993) studied Anglicans, with a sample of 116 individuals. The data revealed preferences for introversion (62%) over extraversion (38%), for intuition (64%) over sensing (36%), for feeling (69%) over thinking (31%), and for judging (59%) over perceiving (41%). Ross (1995) studied Anglophone Roman Catholics, with a sample of 175 individuals. The data were analysed by sex. The women displayed preferences for introversion (53%) over extraversion (47%), for sensing (54%) over intuition (46%), for feeling (75%) over thinking (25%), and for judging (61%) over perceiving (39%). The men displayed preferences for introversion (54%) over extraversion (46%), for thinking (59%) over feeling (41%), for judging (59%) over perceiving (41%), and a balance between sensing (51%) and intuition (49%).

Some important and straightforward clues emerge from these Canadian studies. All five samples reported preferences for introversion and for judging. Catholic, Protestant and Anglican congregations in Canada all find it easier to attract introverts rather than extraverts, and to attract judging types rather than perceiving types. Here is a style of congregation in which extraverts and perceiving types might feel less immediately at home.

Research into the psychological type profile of church members in England was initiated by Francis, Butler, Jones and Craig (2004) among a sample of 158 individuals, and extended by Francis, Duncan, Craig and Luffman (2004) among a sample of 327 individuals. Both studies were based on Anglicans and lead to similar conclusions. The present discussion will concentrate on the larger of these two studies.

In the study reported by Francis, Duncan, Craig and Luffman (2004), the Myers-Briggs Type Indicator (Myers and McCaulley, 1985) was systematically administered throughout the worshippers in five typical Anglican congregations. Four of the congregations were in the Diocese of Manchester and one was in the Diocese of York. Useable responses were received from 116 men and 211 women. The individual congregations provided 87, 70, 65, 56, and 49 participants.

Of the total male respondents from whom data on age were available, 4% were under the age of thirty, 24% were in their thirties, 20% were in their forties, 19% were in their fifties, and 33% were aged sixty or over. Of the total female respondents from whom data on age were available, 3% were under the age of twenty, 7% were in their twenties, 19% were in their thirties, 15% were in their forties, 19% were in their fifties, and 37% were aged sixty or over.

This study found that among the women there were preferences for introversion (55%) over extraversion (45%), for sensing (74%) over intuition (26%), for feeling (73%) over thinking (27%), and for judging (67%) over perceiving (33%). Among the men there were preferences for introversion (66%) over extraversion (34%), for sensing (68%) over intuition (32%), and for judging (70%) over perceiving (30%). The balance was close between feeling (48%) and thinking (52%). Among the women ISFJ accounted for 21% of all the worshippers. Among the men ISTJ accounted for 27% of all the worshippers.

On the basis of the evidence currently available, we need to try to assess the implications of the research findings for church life. Since the information available in the United Kingdom is limited to Anglican congregations this analysis will be conducted from an Anglican perspective. Further replication studies are needed to extend these findings among other denominations.

Introversion or extraversion

In the study reported by Francis, Duncan, Craig and Luffman (2004) both male and female members of Anglican congregations expressed a preference for introversion over extraversion. This finding is consistent with seven previous studies, conducted among Unitarian Universalists (Gerhardt, 1983), Evangelical Protestants (Delis-Bulhoes, 1990), Roman Catholics (Delis-Bulhoes, 1990; Ross, 1995), Anglicans (Ross, 1993) and active Evangelical Lutherans (Rehak, 1998). A range of different denominations across different cultures appear to attract a higher proportion of introverts.

EXERCISE

Why do Anglican congregations appeal more to introverts than to extraverts? What is it about Anglicanism, or about Christian churches more generally, that may attract introverts more than extraverts? What are the strengths and weaknesses of this situation?

The finding that Anglican churches appeal more to introverts than to extraverts is consistent with the view that the dominant spirituality fostered by the western Christian tradition is one which promotes and values the inward journey and may encourage the inward discipline of personal prayer, 'quiet times', and communion with God. In essence this is an introverted faith. According to the data Anglican churches in England are not alone in nurturing and retaining introverted members. The bigger challenge, however, seems to be that of sharing the faith with extraverts.

Recognising that the predominant style of Anglican congregations is shaped to favour an introverted approach to spirituality may have significant implications for those appointed to lead such congregations. On the positive side, there is much in the Anglican tradition for introverts to value, including quiet and meditative services, like the early morning Holy Communion and the service of Evensong. Introverts are more likely to appreciate silence both before services and during services, the opportunity to prepare for worship beforehand, and being provided with written information. Introverts are less likely to welcome interactive teaching techniques in sermons, exchanging the peace during the service, or overemphasis on social events. Extravert leaders who come to take charge of introvert congregations may well be puzzled as to why their plans to develop the social life of the church are so difficult to realise.

Sensing or intuition

In the study reported by Francis, Duncan, Craig and Luffman (2004) both male and female members of Anglican congregations expressed a clear preference for sensing over intuition. Preference for sensing was shown in three studies among Evangelical Protestants (Delis-Bulhoes, 1990) and Roman Catholics (Delis-Bulhoes, 1990; Ross, 1995), while preference for intuition was shown in two studies among Unitarian Universalists (Gerhardt, 1983) and Anglicans (Ross, 1993). Among active Evangelical Lutherans (Rehak, 1998) and male Roman Catholics (Ross, 1995) there was an equal balance between sensing and intuition. Such findings tend to suggest that some types of churches may minister more effectively among sensing types, while other types of churches may minister more effectively among intuitive types. In this situation, Anglicanism veers toward a preference for sensing.

EXERCISE

Why do Anglican congregations appeal more to sensing types than to intuitive types? What is it about Anglicanism that may attract sensing types more than intuitive types? What are the strengths and weaknesses of this situation?

The finding that Anglican churches appeal more to sensing types than to intuitive types suggests that Anglicanism in England may be more accessible to individuals who prefer tradition rather than innovation and change. The bigger challenge, however, seems to be that of sharing faith with intuitive types.

Recognising that the predominant style of Anglican congregations is shaped to favour a sensing approach to spirituality may have significant implications for those appointed to lead such congregations. On the positive side, there is much in the Anglican tradition for sensing types to value, including tradition, familiarity and predictable repetition. Sensing types are likely to appreciate well-known hymns, well-established liturgy, and keeping to well-tried schedules. Sensing types are less likely to welcome change, experimentation, new music and new service books. Intuitive leaders who come to take charge of sensing congregations may well be puzzled as to why their visions for change and development are so difficult to realise.

Thinking or feeling

In the study reported by Francis, Duncan, Craig and Luffman (2004) female members of Anglican congregations expressed a preference for feeling over thinking. Among male members of Anglican congregations a different picture emerges. Among men there is a balance between thinking and feeling. When men and women are considered together, however, these data suggest that Anglican congregations are heavily weighted toward feeling. Females outnumber males in Anglican congregations by about two to one (Francis, 1997) and according to the present study three out of every four women in the congregation prefer feeling. Preference for feeling was shown in four previous studies, conducted among Roman Catholics (Delis-Bulhoes, 1990), Roman Catholic females (Ross, 1995), Anglicans (Ross, 1993) and Evangelical Lutherans (Rehak, 1998). Preference for thinking was shown in the type tables published for Roman Catholic males (Ross, 1995) and

Evangelical Protestants (Delis-Bulhoes, 1990). Among Unitarian Universalists the balance was equal between thinking and feeling (Gerhardt, 1983). Such findings tend to suggest that some types of churches may minister more effectively among feeling types, while other types of churches may minister more effectively among thinking types. In this situation, Anglicanism veers toward a preference for feeling.

EXERCISE

Why do Anglican congregations appeal more to feeling types than to thinking types? What is it about Anglicanism that may attract feeling types more than thinking types? What are the strengths and weaknesses of this situation?

The finding that Anglican churches appeal more to feeling types than to thinking types is consistent with the image that a significant component of the Christian tradition focuses on inter-personal values, harmony and peace. In essence this is a feeling faith. The data suggest that the Anglican churches in England are highly successful in nurturing women who prefer a feeling type spirituality. The bigger challenge, however, seems to be that of accommodating men within the congregation. Men, it would seem, are a minority in Anglicanism, not only in terms of their sex, but also in terms of their psychological preference for thinking rather than for feeling.

Recognising that the predominant style of Anglican congregations is shaped to favour a feeling approach to spirituality may have significant implications for those appointed to lead such congregations. On the positive side, there is much in the Anglican tradition to nurture a theology grounded in inter-relational values, in care and concern for one another, and in harmony and peace. Feeling types are likely to appreciate a church which knows how to compromise in order to avoid conflict and which embraces diversity of opinion without forcing absolute judgements. Feeling types are less likely to welcome doctrinal and moral absolutes which exclude others, and management techniques which place institutional goals above individual welfare. Thinking leaders who come to take charge of feeling congregations may well be puzzled as to why their clear commitment to objective truth and justice may so often fail to win the hearts and souls of the core membership.

Judging and perceiving

In the study reported by Francis, Duncan, Craig and Luffman (2004) both male and female members of Anglican congregations expressed a preference for judging over perceiving. This finding is consistent with seven previous studies, conducted among Unitarian Universalists (Gerhardt, 1983), Evangelical Protestants (Delis-Bulhoes, 1990), Roman Catholics (Delis-Bulhoes, 1990; Ross, 1995), Anglicans (Ross, 1993) and active Evangelical Lutherans (Rehak, 1998). A range of different denominations across different cultures appears to attract a higher proportion of judging types.

EXERCISE

Why do Anglican congregations appeal more to judging types than to perceiving types? What is it about Anglicanism, or about Christian churches more generally, that may attract judging types more than perceiving types? What are the strengths and weaknesses of this situation?

The finding that Anglican churches appeal more to judging types than to perceiving types is consistent with the view that the dominant framework promoted by church services is one which values structure, pattern and discipline. In essence this is a judging faith. According to the data Anglican churches in England are not alone in nurturing and retaining members who prefer judging. The bigger challenge, however, seems to be that of sharing the faith with individuals who prefer perceiving.

Recognising that the predominant style of Anglican congregations is shaped to favour a judging approach to spirituality may have significant implications for those appointed to lead such congregations. On the positive side, there is much in the Anglican tradition to nurture the quest by judging types for form and structure. Judging types are likely to appreciate a church which is tightly governed, services which begin and end on time, and a church diary which is planned well in advance. Judging types are less likely to welcome last minute changes, spontaneous developments, and disruptions to their long-term planning. Perceiving leaders who come to take charge of judging congregations may well be puzzled as to why their spontaneous creativity and productive flexibility are misinterpreted as incompetence and lack of professionalism.

Working with congregational profiles

The type profile of a congregation forms a crucial part of the given context within which adult theological educators need to shape their work, alongside the age profile, the gender distribution, and other key demographic characteristics. Although the type profile may be less easy to observe at first glance than the age profile or gender distribution, it may be of no less significance in defining the spiritual and theological needs of the congregation, or in defining both potential areas for growth and development and areas in which growth is unlikely.

EXERCISE
Imagine that you are responsible for shaping the educational programme of a typical Anglican congregation. How would you use type theory to develop your education strategy? Illustrate your approach to working with the congregation.

There are three constructive ways in which adult theological educators can build on knowledge about the type profile of congregations.

The first strategy is to acknowledge and to respect the strengths of the congregation and to work with those strengths. In the case of a typical Anglican congregation, the strengths are introversion, sensing, feeling and judging (ISFJ). Here, on balance, is a congregation which will prefer an introverted method of learning. Ideas are to be taken away and thought through, not shared immediately and openly discussed. Small groups are preferable to large groups. The task in hand may be of more immediate importance than the social interaction of groups. Here, on balance, is a congregation which will prefer a sensing way of learning, by putting the facts in place before tackling the big picture. For example, in Bible study the text is looked at closely before imaginative links are forged with themes from today's world. Here, on balance, is a congregation which will be more likely to respond initially to the subjective feeling values of the Gospel rather than to the objective thinking aspects. Scripture is first examined for insights into how people relate to God and serve the community, before looking for the theological problems of truth. Here, on balance, is a congregation which will prefer a judging method of learning and works best within fixed parameters. They will appreciate tradition, good order and punctuality.

The second strategy is to enhance the type awareness of the congregation. Type awareness helps individuals to appreciate others by understanding and learning to value how and why they act as they do. In the case of a typical Anglican congregation, those with a strong ISFJ preference need to be able to see their mirror image, ENTP, not as odd or bad, but as different. Given time, the ISFJ congregation can be encouraged to experiment with extravert, intuitive, thinking and perceiving preferences as part of their proper spiritual pilgrimage and development. These are opportunities for the adult theological educator to offer, not conditions to be demanded.

One way of enhancing the type awareness of a congregation is through planned exchanges with another congregation which projects a very different type profile. Sometimes differences between congregations which may appear at first glance to be theologically grounded can, on closer inspection, be better understood in psychological terms. Knowing about type theory may help individuals from very different church traditions to understand and appreciate each other's perspectives in fresh and deeper ways. Knowing about type theory may also help to promote easier acceptance of those who express their faith in God in different and unusual ways.

The third strategy is to identify those members of the congregation who do not conform to the dominant type preference of the congregation. Here are people who may sometimes feel pushed to the margins of their local church life and who may step over the edge into becoming church leavers (Richter and Francis, 1998). It is among such individuals that adult theological educators can begin to form new aspects of local church life, not with the intention of transforming the ISFJ congregation but with the intention of working alongside that congregation. Strong and growing groups within the local church should be welcomed as celebrating God's rich diversity within the human creation, not feared as disrupting congregational homogeneity.

An appreciation of type theory may well lead us to the conclusion that the God who creates such human diversity may also rejoice in the diverse ways in which different congregations celebrate their Christian identity. According to this understanding, the job of the adult theological educator may well be to help individuals find their proper place in the congregation which enables them to give voice to their preferred spiritual life. For example, if the introvert is energised by going on a silent retreat and exhausted by attending a fellowship house party, it may be wise to help the introvert make the most of the retreat tradition. If the extravert is energised by attending a fellowship house party but drained by going on a silent retreat, it may be wise to help the extravert make the most of the house party tradition. The mistake comes when churches try to force God's diverse people into a narrow and stifling conformity.

Conclusion

This chapter has examined the implications of psychological type theory for understanding and leading church congregations. It has argued that type theory may help to explain why some individuals feel less at home than other individuals in certain congregations. The case has been made that a variety of congregational styles may be needed to nurture the spirituality of different psychological type preferences.

Further reading

Baab, L M (1998), *Personality Type in Congregations: how to work with others more effectively*, Washington, DC, Alban Institute.

Duncan, B (1993), *Pray Your Way: your personality and God*, London, Darton, Longman and Todd.

Dwyer, M T (1988), *Wake Up the Sun: an exploration of personality types and spiritual growth*, Thornbury, Victoria, Desbooks.

Edwards, L (1993), *How We Belong, Fight and Pray: the MBTI as a key to congregational dynamics*, Washington DC, Alban Institute.

Faucett, R and Faucett, C A (1987), *Personality and Spiritual Freedom: growing in the Christian life through understanding personality type and the Myers-Briggs Type Indicator*, New York, Doubleday.

Grant, W H, Thompson, M and Clarke, T E (1983), *From Image to Likeness: a Jungian path in the gospel journey*, New York, Paulist Press.

Harbaugh, G, (1990), *God's Gifted People: discovering your personality as a gift*, Minneapolis, Minnesota, Augsburg Publishing House.

Richardson, P T (1996), *Four Spiritualities: expressions of self, expressions of spirit*, Palo Alto, California, Davies-Black.

10. SCRIPTURE, PREACHING AND PSYCHOLOGICAL TYPE

Introduction

Psychological type theory suggests that the way in which different people look at the world is shaped, at least in part, by the development of their dominant function. Dominant sensing types tend to take a particular interest in facts and details. Dominant intuitive types tend to focus on the bigger picture and to spot connections and possibilities. Dominant feeling types tend to focus on matters of human interest, personal relationships and how others feel. Dominant thinking types tend to focus on matters of truth, logic and coherence. It would not be surprising, then, if psychological type had an influence on the way in which different people approach Scripture or on the way in which different preachers proclaimed Scripture from the pulpit.

> ### Reflecting on experience
> Think back over some of the sermons you have heard or think about some of the preachers you have got to know well. Can you detect a preference for sensing, intuition, thinking, or feeling in what you recall?

Biblical hermeneutics

Hermeneutics is concerned with the study of interpretation. There is now a well-established understanding of biblical preaching as hermeneutical dialogue between the text of Scripture and the world-views of both the preacher and the listener (Astley, 2002, 2003). Such an understanding of biblical preaching places weight on critical interrogation both of the text itself and of the worldviews of preacher and listener. The study of these two intellectual activities clearly belongs to very different academic domains. Critical interrogation of the text is properly the professional business of biblical studies. Critical interrogation of the worldviews of preacher and listener is properly the professional business of psychology.

If biblical preaching is indeed to be understood as hermeneutical dialogue of this nature, then there is a good case for the study of preaching to be equally balanced between the professional expertise of biblical studies and the professional expertise of psychology. The balance between these two disciplines in the current debate appears, however, to be heavily weighted in favour of biblical studies.

In an attempt to redress this balance Leslie J Francis and Peter Atkins have attempted to formulate an understanding of Bible study and an understanding of preaching informed by Jung's theory of psychological type. Their understanding is set out clearly in an article entitled 'Psychological type and biblical hermeneutics: SIFT method of preaching' (Francis, 2003). The SIFT method takes seriously the four different perspectives offered by sensing (S), intuition (I), feeling (F) and thinking (T). Writing primarily for an audience well schooled in biblical study and preaching but not so well schooled in Jungian psychology, Francis deliberately chose to represent intuition by I rather than the conventional N.

Psychological perspectives

There is a key psychological principle underpinning the SIFT method of reading Scripture and of preaching. This principle recognises that there is likely to be a deep-rooted and understandable tendency for preachers to preach from their own preferred psychological function. Such preaching may well nurture and stimulate hearers who share the same psychological preference. At the same time, such preaching may fail to engage the interest and attention of those members of the congregation whose perspectives are shaped by a very different psychological preference. Possibly the biggest problem may occur for those listeners whose dominant function coincides with the preacher's inferior function.

I propose now to examine this problem from the perspective of those who sit in the pew. My contention is that sensing, intuitive, thinking and feeling types all come to the sermon with different expectations and different needs. Sometimes these expectations and needs are met by the preacher and sometimes they are ignored.

When *sensing types* hear a passage of Scripture, they want to savour all the detail of the text and may become fascinated by descriptions that appeal to their senses. They tend to start from a fairly literal interest in what is being said.

Sensing types may want to find out all they can about the passage and about the facts that stand behind the passage. They welcome preachers who lead them into the passage by repeating the story and by giving them time to observe and appreciate the details.

It is the intuitive preacher who is most likely to disappoint the sensing types sitting in the congregation. Sensing types quickly lose the thread if they are bombarded with too many possibilities too quickly.

When *intuitive types* hear a passage of Scripture they want to know how that passage will fire their imagination and stimulate their ideas. They tend to focus not on the literal meaning of what is being said, but on the possibilities and challenges implied.

Intuitive types may want to explore all of the possible directions in which the passage could lead. They welcome preachers who throw out suggestions and brainstorm possibilities, whether or not these are obviously linked to the passage, and whether or not these ideas are followed through.

It is the sensing preacher who is most likely to disappoint the intuitive types sitting in the congregation. Intuitive types quickly become bored with too much detail, too many facts and too much repetition.

When *feeling types* hear a passage of Scripture they want to know what the passage has to say about personal values and about human relationships. They empathise deeply with people in the story and with the human drama in the narrative.

Feeling types are keen to get inside the lives of people about whom they hear in Scripture. They want to explore what it felt like to be there at the time and how those feelings help to illuminate their Christian journey today. They welcome preachers who take time to develop the human dimension of the passage and who apply the passage to issues of compassion, harmony and trust.

It is the thinking preacher who is most likely to disappoint the feeling types sitting in the congregation. Feeling types quickly lose interest in theological debates which explore abstract issues without clear application to personal relationships.

When *thinking types* hear a passage of Scripture they want to know what the passage has to say about principles of truth and justice. They get caught up with the principles involved in the story and with the various kinds of truth claims being made.

Thinking types are often keen to do theology and to follow through the implications and the logic of the positions they adopt. Some thinking types apply this perspective to a literal interpretation of Scripture, while other thinking types are more at home with the liberal interpretation of Scripture. They welcome preachers who are fully alert to the logical and to the theological implications of their themes. They value sermons which debate fundamental issues of integrity and righteousness.

It is the feeling preacher who is most likely to disappoint the thinking types sitting in the congregation. Thinking types quickly lose interest in sermons which concentrate on applications to personal relationships, but fail to debate critically issues of theology and morality.

EXERCISE
Draw on what you know about your psychological preferences and your experience of listening to sermons or studying the Bible. What really catches your attention in a sermon? What really loses your attention in a sermon?

Theological perspectives

The SIFT method of preaching is not simply an attempt to challenge preachers to recognise the impact of their own psychological preferences on their approach to Scripture and on their preaching style. The SIFT method of preaching is much more theologically informed and theologically alert than that. By recognising the distinctive voices of the four psychological functions, the SIFT method of preaching sets out to engage Scripture from all four perspectives in a disciplined and systematic way. If biblical preaching is indeed to be understood as hermeneutical dialogue between the text and the listener, then all of the listener's psychological functions need to be properly engaged in that dialogue.

In an attempt to test and to establish the SIFT method of preaching, Leslie J Francis and Peter Atkins (2000, 2001, 2002) worked systematically through the principal gospel readings set out in the Revised Common Lectionary in their three books, *Exploring Matthew's Gospel*, *Exploring Mark's Gospel* and *Exploring Luke's Gospel*. They approach each gospel reading from the perspective of Jung's four primary psychological processes: sensing, intuition, feeling and thinking. Each preaching event takes all four perspectives and does so in a recognised fixed order of progression.

There are two main, interrelated but distinct theological reasons behind this approach. The first theological reason is grounded in an application of individual differences. It is recognised that different individuals in the congregation will be able to relate more easily to one of these four functions than to the other three. Faith in a God who creates diversity and who rejoices in individual differences demands that each psychological type should be properly included and embraced in the act of preaching.

The second theological reason is grounded in an appreciation of the quest for wholeness and completeness. Although each individual may prefer (and therefore develop) one of the four functions, human development presses toward properly embracing and developing all four. It is precisely in humanity's encounter with the creator God revealed through the text of Scripture that the individual is challenged to love God with *all* his or her mind: with sensing, with intuition, with feeling and with thinking.

The first step in the SIFT method is to address the sensing perspective. It is the sensing perspective which gets to grip with the text itself and which gives proper attention to the insights of biblical scholarship. The first question asks, 'How does this passage speak to the sensing function? What are the facts and details? What is there to see, to hear, to touch, to smell, and to taste?'

The second step in the SIFT method is to address the intuitive perspective. It is the intuitive perspective which relates the biblical text to wider issues and concerns. The second question asks, 'How does this passage speak to the intuitive function? What is there to speak to the imagination, to forge links with current situations, to illuminate issues in our lives?'

The third step in the SIFT method is to address the feeling perspective. It is the feeling perspective which examines the human interest in the biblical text and learns the lessons of God for harmonious and compassionate living. The third question asks, 'How does this passage speak to the feeling function? What is there to speak about fundamental human values, about the relationship between people, and about what it is to be truly human?'

The fourth step in the SIFT method is to address the thinking perspective. It is the thinking perspective which examines the theological interest in the biblical text and which reflects rationally and crucially on issues of principle. The fourth question asks, 'How does this passage speak to the thinking function? What is there to speak to the mind, to challenge us on issues of truth and justice, and to provoke profound theological thinking?'

Studying Scripture

Having introduced the theoretical bases of the SIFT method of preaching, the aim of the second part of this chapter is to test the method in practice. You will be invited to examine four passages from Mark's gospel and to reflect on each passage from *one* psychological perspective. Then an excerpt will be given from Leslie J Francis and Peter Atkins' book, *Exploring Mark's Gospel* (2002) to illustrate how they responded to the same challenges.

Sensing

It is the sensing perspective which gets to grips with the text itself and which gives proper attention to the details of interest to biblical scholarship. The sensing perspective may also wish to lead people into the detail of the story by making full play of the five senses. Here the key value is information.

EXERCISE
📖 **Read Mark 1:40-45.**

Here is Mark's account of Jesus' encounter with the leper. The leper begs Jesus to make him clean. Jesus stretches out his hand and touches the leper, bringing cleansing. Approach this passage from the perspective of the sensing function. Ask the basic sensing questions. What are the facts and details? What is there to see, to hear, to touch, to smell and to taste?

In approaching this passage from a sensing perspective Leslie J Francis and Peter Atkins pay close attention to the details that Mark makes explicit in his text and to the details left implicit but which would be so clearly recognised by the original audience in first-century Palestine. Then Francis and Atkins try to lead the hearers into the power of the narrative by developing their sense of being there at the time. They draw on all the senses of sight, sound, smell, taste, and touch. So hear how a sensing preacher addresses Mark 1:40-45.

Sensing perspective on Mark 1:40-45

Awake from slumber and find yourself transported back in time, back, back to first-century Palestine. You are travelling the dusty road on a warm, warm day. Feel the sun beating down on the back of your neck, taste the dust from the road in the back of your throat, smell the parched atmosphere at the back of your nostrils, and see the scorching road running into the distance, peopled with fellow travellers.

Out there, in the middle of nowhere, your ears prick up and catch a distant sound. You recognise the harsh croak of an untuned voice. You hear an indistinct, but distraught cry. Approaching you along the road is the well-known figure of the leper man.

As the leper man approaches, you see the disfigured unkempt figure. The awful disease has eaten away at self-respect. As the leper man approaches, you hear the distraught cry, 'Unclean, unclean.' The awful disease has eaten away at social relationships and distanced all uncontaminated human contact.

See your fellow travellers avert their eyes and divert their path. Each traveller, in turn, avoids the leper man and reinforces his sense of loneliness, isolation and distance from the human race.

But there, in the crowd, is a fellow traveller who disobeys the rules and runs in the face of convention. See Jesus of Nazareth stretch out his hand to touch the leper man who is himself untouchable. Hear the gasp of surprise, the gasp of incredulity, the gasp of horror, as Jesus makes himself unclean by such intimate contact with the leper man, whose disease is so readily communicable, physically, socially and ritually.

See Jesus take up the leper man's cry and shout out his own pollution. See the leper man lay down his leprosy, peel away his disfigurement, slough off his social isolation, and make his way to the priest to proclaim the cleansing and rehabilitation so freely offered.

You have been transported back in time, back, back to first-century Palestine.

Intuition

It is the intuitive perspective which relates the biblical text to wider issues and concerns and draws links between the world of the text and the world of the hearer. The intuitive perspective looks for spring-boards in the text which spark the imagination and generate new inspired insights. Here the key value is imagination.

EXERCISE
📖 **Read Mark 2:1-12.**

Here is Mark's account of an amazing day in the life of Jesus. Four men come carrying a paralysed man. Because the house where Jesus was staying was so crowded, these four men could get nowhere near him. So they broke up the roof and lowered the stretcher down. The paralysed man was healed. Approach this passage from the perspective of the intuitive function. Just brain-storm the links and the possibilities. What ideas come to mind? What gets sparked in your imagination? What is God saying through the text?

In approaching this passage from an intuitive perspective, Leslie J Francis and Peter Atkins light on four different themes. The passage sparks ideas about collaborative ministry, about the discipline of intercessory prayer, about individuals' responsibility for their own salvation, and about the Christian vocation to serve without seeking reward. Can you see how all these ideas can be sparked by the same story? Can you imagine how whole sermons can be preached on each of these themes? So hear how an intuitive preacher reflects on Mark 2:1-12.

Intuitive perspective on Mark 2:1-12
Here is a story about four people who brought their friend to Jesus. They were unaffected by the encounter themselves, but their friend's life was changed. So where does that leave you and me?

We, too, are called to bring others to Jesus. It is often not an easy task when we are working in isolation, one by one. Just one of the friends would never have got the paralysed man as far as the threshold. Four of them together raised the paralysed man to the rooftop and delivered him at the feet of Jesus. Collaborative ministry may achieve what individual ministry fails to do.

We, too, are called to bring others to Jesus. It is often no easy task to bundle our candidates on to a stretcher and to lug them lock, stock and barrel into the presence of Jesus. But we can, at least, begin by carrying them to the Lord day by day in prayer. And this may be more effective than carrying them to the rooftop of the church. The ministry of prayer may achieve what the ambulance ministry fails to do.

We, too, are called to bring others to Jesus. But note carefully, our calling stops right there. The real work takes place face to face, between Jesus and the candidate. We cannot negotiate healing and salvation on their behalf. In the story, the paralysed man takes responsibility for his own condition. He stood on his own two feet and accepted the gift of mobility.

We, too, are called to bring others to Jesus. But we must always be willing to do so for their benefit and not for our own. In the story, when the healing was complete, the four men vanished from the narrative, thanked neither by Jesus nor by the man who had been healed. They had performed their task and were happy to return to their home. We can only hope that they had the courtesy to repair the roof before they left.

Here is a story about four people who brought their friend to Jesus. Pray that we may continue to do the same.

Feeling

It is the feeling perspective which examines the human interest in the biblical text and which tries to learn the lessons of God for harmonious and compassionate human living. The feeling perspective searches the text to hear about human values, about the relationships between people, and about what it is to be truly human. Here the key value is empathy.

EXERCISE
📖 Read Mark 1:29-39.

Here is Mark's description of Jesus' visit to the house of Simon and Andrew, where he finds Simon's mother-in-law in bed with a fever. Approach this part of the passage from the perspective of the feeling function. Try to get alongside one of the key characters. Try to establish empathy with what is happening in the house. What can you feel about the hopes and fears, about the tensions and problems, about the human joy and happiness of that household?

In approaching this passage from a feeling perspective, Leslie J Francis and Peter Atkins select one of the characters and recreate the experience from that individual's point of view. Having tried first to step into the shoes of the more obvious characters in the story (Simon, Jesus, and the sick mother-in-law), they prefer to adopt the perspective of the person who was crucial to the whole story but utterly marginalised by the gospel writer, namely Simon's wife and daughter of the sick mother-in-law. So hear how a feeling preacher reflects on Mark 1:29-39.

Feeling perspective on Mark 1:29-39

Here is a tale of family life. Try to see it through the eyes of the woman whom Mark excluded from the tale. Grasp how things feel from the daughter's perspective, from the perspective of Simon's wife. Put yourself in the unenviable place of the woman caught between mother and husband. Feel that conflict in her soul.

The daughter's loyalty to her mother is deep and true. It is hard to forget the sacrifices the mother made in bringing up her family. After all, times were bad and life was hard for the wife of the Galilean fisherman. Once the daughter was totally dependent on the mother. But now the tables are turned. Late, late in life, the mother is now totally dependent on the daughter. Once her husband brought home the fish, but now the home economy is supported by her daughter's husband.

How can a daughter loyal to her mother's needs see her way of life, her very security threatened by a radical change in the home economy?

How can a daughter but sympathise with a mother who retreats to bed in protest or confusion?

The wife's loyalty to her husband is deep and true as well. It is hard to forget the deep felt love and tenderness which first attracted her to the young fisherman. After all, there had been many fish in the local sea. But the choice had been made and there had been, until now, little reason to regret it. Simon had supported her and her mother, too, through days when fish were plentiful and through days when fish were scarce.

How can a wife loyal to her husband's needs stand in the way, when he hears and responds to the call of God? How can a wife but understand when her husband takes time out to build the kingdom of God?

Here, then, is a tale of family life. Try to see it through the eyes of the woman whom Mark excluded from the tale. Put yourself in the unenviable place of the woman caught between mother and husband. Empathise with the deep conflict in her soul.

Thinking

It is the thinking perspective which examines the theological interest in the biblical text and which reflects rationally and critically on issues of principle. The thinking perspective searches the text to provoke profound theological reflection. Here the key value is truth.

EXERCISE
📖 **Read Mark 1:14-20.**

Here is Mark's description of Jesus' first actions after his baptism and period in the wilderness. Here are the first recorded acts of Jesus' public ministry in Mark's gospel. Approach the passage from the perspective of the thinking function. What issues are raised in your mind about the structure of Mark's gospel, and about Mark's intention in starting the story where he does? What theological issues are raised by the passage?

In approaching this passage from a thinking perspective, Leslie J Francis and Peter Atkins employ some recognised tools of New

Testament theology. They are interested in trying to get inside the mind of the gospel writer Mark and to identify his theological interests. Their analysis is that Mark begins the gospel narrative with the call of the disciples because his primary theological interest is in showing how Jesus established a new Israel. The old Israel was founded as twelve tribes, with the Levites sometimes counted as the thirteenth tribe. In the same way Jesus calls and names twelve disciples, with Levi called but not counted among the twelve. So hear how a thinking preacher reflects on Mark 1:14-20.

Thinking perspective on Mark 1:14-20

The key question for the theologian concerned with gospel studies is this. Why did Mark choose to open his gospel narrative with the account of the call of four disciples, rather than by relating some of the words of teaching or the acts of healing which would logically lead to people wishing to follow him?

The answer is that this opening call set the *structure* for what is to follow. Mark's primary interest is in showing how Jesus constructed around him a new Israel, a new people of God. The clue is given by the way in which the call of the first four followers (Peter, Andrew, James and John) is followed by the call of a fifth follower (Levi). Then there is a general commissioning of the twelve special disciples. The twelve are named and Levi is dropped from the list. The same thing, you see, so often happens in the Old Testament when the twelve tribes of Israel are named. There, too, Levi is often dropped from the list and the number twelve is kept alive by counting separately the two sons of Joseph, namely Ephraim and Manasseh. Mark's intention is clear.

For Mark, the words of teaching and the acts of healing are not there to attract the twelve followers, but to equip them. The teaching and the healing are the object lessons from which they are to learn. Then having learnt, they themselves are sent out to teach and to heal, the very activities which bear witness to the fact that the Kingdom of God has come near. Where God reigns, the words of the Kingdom and the new life of the Kingdom are free for all to receive.

For Mark, therefore, the call of the first disciples is, indeed, the proper opening act for the Jesus who comes proclaiming, 'The time is fulfilled, and the Kingdom of God has come near.'

Conclusion

This chapter has examined the implications of psychological type theory for the study of Scripture and for preaching. It has done so by introducing the SIFT method of preaching, a method developed on the basis of three principles. The first principle is that an understanding of biblical preaching as a hermeneutical dialogue between the text of Scripture and the worldviews of preacher and listener properly involves the discipline of psychology as a key tool in the analysis and development of the place of preaching in the Christian community. The second principle is that the Jungian notion of psychological type provides an insightful and accessible model of the human psyche which is of practical relevance to the preaching process. The third principle is that there is good theological justification for the preaching event to address all four of the psychological functions identified by Jung in response to the first of the great commandments to love the Lord God with all our heart, with all our soul, and with *all our mind.*

Further reading

Astley, J (2002), *Ordinary Theology: looking, listening and learning theology,* Aldershot, Ashgate.

Francis, L J and Atkins, P (2000), *Exploring Luke's Gospel: a guide to the gospel readings in the Revised Common Lectionary,* London, Mowbray.

Francis, L J and Atkins, P (2001), *Exploring Matthew's Gospel: a guide to the gospel readings in the Revised Common Lectionary,* London, Mowbray.

Francis, L J and Atkins, P (2002), *Exploring Mark's Gospel: an aid for readers and preachers using year B of the Revised Common Lectionary,* London, Continuum.

Grant, W H, Thompson, M and Clarke, T E (1983), *From Image to Likeness: a Jungian path in the gospel journey,* New York, Paulist Press.

Innes, R (1996), *Personality Indicators and the Spiritual Life,* Cambridge, Grove Books.

Johnson, R (1995), *Your Personality and the Spiritual Life,* Crowbridge, Monarch.

Martínez, P (2001), *Prayer Life: how your personality affects the way you pray,* Carlisle, Paternoster.

APPENDIX

Francis Psychological Type Scales (FPTS)

The copyright of this questionnaire is vested in Leslie J Francis. Users of this book may make copies of the questionnaire for their own personal use in order to explore the application of psychological type for faith. For all other purposes written permission must be obtained from the copyright holder by writing to:

Professor Leslie J Francis
Welsh National Centre for Religious Education
University of Wales, Bangor
Normal Site (Meirion)
Bangor
Gwynedd LL57 2PX
UK

The following list contains pairs of characteristics. For each pair tick (✓) **ONE** box next to that characteristic which is **closer** to the real you, even if you feel both characteristics apply to you. Tick the characteristic that reflects the real you, even if other people see you differently.

PLEASE COMPLETE EVERY QUESTION

Do you tend to be more . . .
active   **or**   reflective

Do you tend to be more . . .
interested in facts   **or**   interested in theories

Do you tend to be more . . .
concerned for harmony   **or**   concerned for justice

Do you tend to be more . . .
happy with routine   **or**   unhappy with routine

Are you more . . .
private   **or**   sociable

Are you more . . .
inspirational   **or**   practical

Are you more . . .
analytic   **or**   sympathetic

Are you more . . .
structured   **or**   open-ended

Do you prefer . . .
having many friends   **or**   a few deep friendships

Do you prefer . . .
the concrete   **or**   the abstract

Do you prefer . . .
feeling   **or**   thinking

Do you prefer . . .
to act on impulse   **or**   to act on decisions

Do you . . .
dislike parties   **or**   like parties

Do you . . .
prefer to design   **or**   prefer to make

Do you . . .
tend to be firm   **or**   tend to be gentle

Do you . . .
like to be in control   **or**   like to be adaptable

Are you . . .
energised by others   **or**   drained by too many people

Are you . . .
conventional   **or**   inventive

Are you . . .
critical   **or**   affirming

Are you . . .
happier working alone   **or**   happier working in groups

Do you tend to be more . . .
socially detached   **or**   socially involved

Do you tend to be more . . .
concerned for meaning   **or**   concerned about detail

Do you tend to be more . . .
logical   **or**   humane

Do you tend to be more . . .
orderly   **or**   easygoing

Are you more . . .
talkative   **or**   reserved

Are you more . . .
sensible   **or**   imaginative

Are you more . . .
tactful   **or**   truthful

Are you more . . .
    spontaneous   **or**   organised

Are you mostly . . .
    an introvert   **or**   an extravert

Are you mostly focused on . . .
    present realities   **or**   future possibilities

Are you mostly . . .
    trusting   **or**   sceptical

Are you mostly . . .
    leisurely   **or**   punctual

Do you . . .
    speak before thinking   **or**   think before speaking

Do you prefer to . . .
    improve things   **or**   keep things as they are

Do you . . .
    seek for truth   **or**   seek for peace

Do you . . .
    dislike detailed planning   **or**   like detailed planning

Are you . . .
    happier with uncertainty   **or**   happier with certainty

Are you . . .
    up in the air   **or**   down to earth

Are you . . .
    warm-hearted   **or**   fair-minded

Are you . . .
    systematic   **or**   casual

REFERENCES

Allport, G W (1950), *The Individual and his Religion*, New York, Macmillan.

Argyle, M (1958), *Religious Behaviour*, London, Routledge and Kegan Paul.

Argyle, M and Beit-Hallahmi, B (1975), *The Social Psychology of Religion*, London, Routledge and Kegan Paul.

Astley, J (2002), *Ordinary Theology: looking, listening and learning theology*, Aldershot, Ashgate.

Astley, J (2003), 'Ordinary theology for rural theology and rural ministry', *Rural Theology*, 1, 3–12.

Astley, J and Francis, L J (eds) (1992), *Christian Perspectives on Faith Development: a reader*, Leominster, Fowler Wright and Grand Rapids, Michigan, Eerdmans.

Bayne, R (1995), *The Myers-Briggs Type Indicator: a critical review and practical guide*, London, Chapman and Hall.

Beit-Hallahmi, B and Argyle, M (1997), *The Psychology of Religious Belief and Experience*, London, Routledge.

Bents, R and Wierschke, A (1996), 'Test-retest reliability of the Myers-Briggs Typenindikator', *Journal of Psychological Type*, 36, 42–46.

Bourke, R, Francis, L J and Robbins, M (2004), *Cattell's personality model and attitude toward Christianity* (in press).

Bradley, J (1986), 'Personality or performance?', *Nursing Times*, 82(20), 45–46.

Budd, R J (1997), *Manual for Jung Type Indicator*, Bedford, Psytech International.

Cattell, R B (1986), 'The 16PF personality structure and Dr Eysenck', *Journal of Social Behaviour and Personality*, 1, 153–160.

Cattell, R B, Cattell, A K S and Cattell, H E P (1993), *Sixteen Personality Factor Questionnaire: fifth edition (16PF5)*, Windsor, NFER-Nelson.

Cattell, R B, Cattell, M D L and Johns E F (1984), *Manual and Norms for the High School Personality Questionnaire: the HSPQ*, Champaign, Illinois, Institute for Personality and Ability Testing.

Cattell, R B, Eber, H W and Tatsuoka, M M (1970), *Handbook for the Sixteen Personality Factor Questionnaire (16PF)*, Champaign, Illinois, Institute for Personality and Ability Testing.

Corulla, W J (1990), 'A revised version of the psychoticism scale for children', *Personality and Individual Differences*, 11, 65–76.

Costa, P T and McCrae, R R (1985), *The NEO Personality Inventory*, Odessa, Florida, Psychological Assessment Resources.

Cowan, D A (1989), 'An alternative to the dichotomous interpretation of Jung's psychological functions: developing more sensitive measurement technology', *Journal of Personality Assessment*, 53, 459–471.

Coxon, T (1996), Fads and foibles in the contemporary church, in K Leech (ed.), *Myers-Briggs: some critical reflections*, pp. 2–6, Croydon, The Jubilee Group.

Craig, C, Francis, L J and Robbins, M (2004), 'Psychological type and sex differences among church leaders in the United Kingdom', *Journal of Beliefs and Values* (in press).

Cranton, P and Knoop, R (1995), 'Assessing Jung's psychological types: the PET Type Check', *Genetic, Social and General Psychology Monographs*, 121, 249–274.

Cronbach, L J (1951), 'Coefficient alpha and the internal structure of tests', *Psychometrika*, 16, 297–334.

Davies, J (1996), Psychometrics: measurement or mythology?, in K Leech (ed.), *Myers-Briggs: some critical reflections*, pp. 19–23, Croydon, The Jubilee Group.

Delis-Bulhoes, V (1990), 'Jungian psychological types and Christian belief in active church members', *Journal of Psychological Type*, 20, 25–33.

Delmerge, A (1996), On the usefulness of personality testing for 'being', in K Leech (ed.), *Myers-Briggs: some critical reflections*, pp. 35–38, Croydon, The Jubilee Group.

De Vellis, R F (2003), *Scale Development: theory and applications*, London, Sage.

Descouzis, D P (1989), 'Psychological types of tax preparers', *Journal of Psychological Type*, 17, 36–38.

Dittes, J E (1971), Psychological characteristics of religious professionals, in M Strommen (ed.), *Research on Religious Development: a comprehensive handbook*, pp. 422–460, New York, Hawthorn Books Inc.

Egan, A (1996), Myers-Briggs and religious life: reflections from experience, in K Leech (ed.), *Myers-Briggs: some critical reflections*, pp. 28–31, Croydon, The Jubilee Group.

Ellis, A (1962), *The Case Against Religion*, New York, Institute for Rational Living.

Evans, W (1986), 'Personality and stress', *Personality and Individual Differences*, 7, 251–253.

Eysenck, H J (1952), *The Scientific Study of Personality*, London, Routledge and Kegan Paul.

Eysenck, H J (1959), *Manual for the Maudsley Personality Inventory*, London, University of London Press.

Eysenck, H J (1967), *The Biological Basis of Personality*, Springfield, Illinois, Charles Thomas.

Eysenck, H J (1972), 'Primaries or second-order factors: a critical consideration of Cattell's 16PF battery', *British Journal of Social and Clinical Psychology*, 11, 265–269.

Eysenck, H J (1991), 'Dimensions of personality, 16, 5 or 3? Criteria for a taxonomic paradigm', *Personality and Individual Differences*, 12, 773–790.

Eysenck, H J and Eysenck, M W (1985), *Personality and Individual Differences: a natural science approach*, New York, Plenum Press.

Eysenck, H J and Eysenck, S B G (1964), *Manual of the Eysenck Personality Inventory*, London, University of London Press.

Eysenck, H J and Eysenck, S B G (1975), *Manual of the Eysenck Personality Questionnaire (adult and junior)*, London, Hodder and Stoughton.

Eysenck, H J and Eysenck, S B G (1976), *Psychoticism as a Dimension of Personality*, London, Hodder and Stoughton.

Eysenck, H J and Eysenck, S B G (1991), *Manual of the Eysenck Personality Scales*, London, Hodder and Stoughton.

Eysenck, S B G (1965), *Manual of the Junior Eysenck Personality Inventory*, London, University of London Press.

Eysenck, S B G, Eysenck, H J and Barrett, P (1985), 'A revised version of the psychoticism scale', *Personality and Individual Differences*, 6, 21–29.

Fowler, J W (1981), *Stages of Faith: the psychology of human development and the quest for meaning*, San Francisco, California, Harper and Row.

Francis, L J (1991a), 'The dual nature of the EPQ lie scale among college students in England', *Personality and Individual Differences*, 12, 1255–1260.

Francis, L J (1991b), 'The personality characteristics of Anglican ordinands: feminine men and masculine women?', *Personality and Individual Differences*, 12, 1133–1140.

Francis, L J (1992), 'Is psychoticism really a dimension of personality fundamental to religiosity?', *Personality and Individual Differences*, 13, 645–652.

Francis, L J (1993), 'The dual nature of the Eysenckian neuroticism scales: a question of sex differences?', *Personality and Individual Differences*, 15, 43–59.

Francis, L J (1996), 'The development of an abbreviated form of the Revised Eysenck Personality Questionnaire (JEPQR-A) among 13–15 year olds', *Personality and Individual Differences*, 21, 835–844.

Francis, L J (1997), 'The psychology of gender differences in religion: a review of empirical research', *Religion*, 27, 81–96.

Francis, L J (2002), 'Personality theory and empirical theology', *Journal of Empirical Theology*, 15, 37–53.

Francis, L J (2003), 'Psychological type and biblical hermeneutics: SIFT method of preaching', *Rural Theology*, 1, 13–23.

Francis, L J (2004a), Prayer, personality and purpose in life among churchgoing and non-churchgoing adolescents, in L J Francis, M Robbins and J Astley (eds), *Religion, Education and Adolescence: international empirical perspectives*, Cardiff, University of Wales Press (in press).

Francis, L J (2004b), *Francis Psychological Type Scales (FPTS): technical manual*, Bangor, Welsh National Centre for Religious Education.

Francis, L J (2004c), 'Psychological types of female trainee primary school teachers in Wales: teaching in a changing educational climate', *Journal of Psychological Type* (in press).

Francis, L J and Atkins, P (2000), *Exploring Luke's Gospel: a guide to the gospel readings in the Revised Common Lectionary*, London, Mowbray.

Francis, L J and Atkins, P (2001), *Exploring Matthew's Gospel: a guide to the gospel readings in the Revised Common Lectionary*, London, Mowbray.

Francis, L J and Atkins, P (2002), *Exploring Mark's Gospel: an aid for readers and preachers using year B of the Revised Common Lectionary*, London, Continuum.

Francis, L J and Bourke, R (2004), 'Personality and religion: applying Cattell's model among secondary school pupils', *Current Psychology* (in press).

Francis, L J., Brown, L B. and Philipchalk, R (1992), 'The development of an abbreviated form of the Revised Eysenck Personality Questionnaire (EPQR-A): its use among students in England, Canada, the USA and Australia', *Personality and Individual Differences*, 13, 443–449.

Francis, L J, Butler, A, Jones, S H and Craig, C L (2004), 'Type patterns among active members of the Anglican church: a perspective from England', *Mental Health, Religion and Culture* (in press).

Francis, L J, Craig, C L and Butler, A (2004), 'Psychological types of male evangelical Anglican seminarians in England', *Journal of Psychological Type* (in press).

Francis, L J, Duncan, B, Craig, C L and Luffman, G (2004), 'Type patterns among Anglican congregations in England', *Journal of Adult Theological Education* (in press).

Francis, L J and Jones, S H (eds) (1996), *Psychological Perspectives on Christian Ministry: a reader*, Leominster, Gracewing.

Francis, L J, Jones, S H and Wilcox, C (2000), 'Religiosity and happiness: during adolescence, young adulthood and later life', *Journal of Psychology and Christianity*, 19, 245–257.

Francis, L J and Kay, W K (1995), 'The personality characteristics of Pentecostal ministry candidates', *Personality and Individual Differences*, 18, 581–594.

Francis, L J, Lewis, J M, Brown, L B, Philipchalk, R and Lester, D (1995), 'Personality and religion among undergraduate students in the United Kingdom, United States, Australia and Canada', *Journal of Psychology and Christianity*, 14, 250–262.

Francis, L J, Lewis, J M, Philipchalk, R, Brown, L B, and Lester, D (1995), 'The internal consistency reliability and construct validity of the Francis Scale of Attitude toward Christianity (adult) among undergraduate students in the UK, USA, Australia and Canada', *Personality and Individual Differences*, 19, 949–953.

Francis, L J and Musson, D J (1999), 'Male and female Anglican clergy in England: gender reversal on the 16PF?', *Journal of Empirical Theology*, 12(2), 5–16.

Francis, L J and Payne, V J (2002), 'The Payne Index of Ministry Styles (PIMS): ministry styles and psychological type among male Anglican clergy in Wales', *Research in the Social Scientific Study of Religion*, 13, 125–141.

Francis, L J, Payne, V J and Jones, S H (2001), 'Psychological types of male Anglican clergy in Wales', *Journal of Psychological Type*, 56, 19–23.

Francis, L J and Pearson, P R (1985a), 'Extraversion and religiosity', *Journal of Social Psychology*, 125, 269–270.

Francis, L J and Pearson, P R (1985b), 'Psychoticism and religiosity among 15 year olds', *Personality and Individual Differences*, 6, 397–398.

Francis, L J and Pearson, P R (1991), 'Religiosity, gender and the two faces of neuroticism', *Irish Journal of Psychology*, 12, 60–68.

Francis, L J, Pearson, P R, Carter, M and Kay, W K (1981a), 'The relationship between neuroticism and religiosity among English 15- and 16-year olds', *Journal of Social Psychology*, 114, 99–102.

Francis, L J, Pearson, P R, Carter, M and Kay, W K (1981b), 'Are introverts more religious?', *British Journal of Social Psychology*, 20, 101–104.

Francis, L J, Pearson, P R and Kay, W K (1983a), 'Neuroticism and religiosity among English school children', *Journal of Social Psychology*, 121, 149–150.

Francis, L J, Pearson, P R and Kay, W K (1983b), 'Are introverts still more religious?', *Personality and Individual Differences*, 4, 211–212.

Francis, L J, Penson, A W and Jones, S H (2001), 'Psychological types of male and female Bible College students in England', *Mental Health, Religion and Culture*, 4, 23–32.

Francis, L J and Robbins, M (1999), *The Long Diaconate: 1987–1994*, Leominster, Gracewing.

Francis, L J and Robbins, M (2004), *Personality and Pastoral Care: a study in empirical theology*, Cambridge, Grove Books.

Francis, R D (1999), *Ethics for Psychologists: a handbook*, Leicester, British Psychological Society.

Freud, S (1950), *The Future of an Illusion*, New Haven, Connecticut, Yale University Press.

Gerhardt, R (1983), 'Liberal religion and personality type', *Research in Psychological Type*, 6, 47–53.

Granleese, J and Barrett, T F (1990), 'The social and personality characteristics of the Irish chartered accountant', *Personality and Individual Differences*, 11, 957–964.

Gray, H and Wheelwright, J B (1946), 'Jung's psychological types, their frequency of occurrence', *Journal of General Psychology*, 34, 3–17.

Gumley, C J G, McKenzie, J, Ormerod, M B and Keys, W (1979), 'Personality correlates in a sample of male nurses in the British Royal Air Force', *Journal of Advanced Nursing*, 4, 355–364.

Harvey, R J (1996), Reliability and validity, in A L Hammer (ed.), *MBTI Applications: a decade of research on the Myers-Briggs Type Indicator*, pp. 5–29, Palo Alto, California, Consulting Psychologists Press.

Harvey, R J and Murry, W D (1994), 'Scoring the Myers-Briggs Type Indicator: empirical comparison of preference score versus latent-trait methods', *Journal of Personality Assessment*, 62, 116–129.

Howes, R J and Carskadon, T G (1979), 'Test-retest reliabilities of the Myers-Briggs Type Indicator as a function of mood changes', *Research in Psychological Type*, 2, 67–72.

Innes, J M and Kitto, S (1989), 'Neuroticism, self-consciousness and coping strategies, and occupational stress in high school teachers', *Personality and Individual Differences*, 10, 303–312.

Jacoby, P F (1981), 'Psychological types and career success in the accounting profession', *Research in Psychological Type*, 4, 24–37.

Johnson, D A (1992), 'Test-retest reliabilities of the Myers-Briggs Type Indicator and the type differentiation indicator over a 30-month period', *Journal of Psychological Type*, 24, 54–58.

Jones, S H and Francis, L J (1997), 'The fate of the Welsh clergy: an attitude survey among male clerics in the Church in Wales', *Contemporary Wales*, 10, 182–199.

Joyce, D (1996), Both feet firmly in the clouds?, in K Leech (ed.), *Myers-Briggs: some critical reflections*, pp. 23–28, Croydon, The Jubilee Group.

Jung, C G (1938), *Psychology and Religion*, New Haven, Connecticut, Yale University Press.

Jung, C G (1971), *Psychological Types: the collected works, volume 6*, London, Routledge and Kegan Paul.

Kay, W K (2000), *Pentecostals in Britain*, Carlisle, Paternoster.

Keirsey, D (1998), *Please Understand Me: 2*, Del Mar, California, Prometheus Nemesis.

Keirsey, D and Bates, M (1978), *Please Understand Me*, Del Mar, California, Prometheus Nemesis.

Kendall, E (1998), *Myers-Briggs Type Indicator: step 1 manual supplement*, Palo Alto, California, Consulting Psychologists Press.

Kier, F J, Melancon, J G and Thompson, B (1998), 'Reliability and validity of scores on the Personal Preferences Self-Description Questionnaire (PPSDQ)', *Educational and Psychological Measurement*, 58, 612–622.

Kitchener, K S (2000), *Foundations of Ethical Practice: research and teaching in psychology*, Mahweh, New Jersey, Lawrence Elbaum Associates.

Kline, P (1993), *The Handbook of Psychological Testing*, London, Routledge.

Lake, F (1966), *Clinical Theology*, London, Darton, Longman and Todd.

Leech, K (ed.) (1996), *Myers-Briggs: some critical reflections*, Croydon, The Jubilee Group.

Levy, N, Murphy, C and Carlson, R (1972), 'Personality types among Negro college students', *Educational and Psychological Measurement*, 32, 641–653.

Loomis, M (1982), 'A new perspective for Jung's typology: the Singer-Loomis Inventory of Personality', *Journal of Analytical Psychology*, 27, 59–69.

Louden, S H and Francis L J (1999), 'The personality profile of Roman Catholic parochial secular priests in England and Wales', *Review of Religious Research*, 41, 65–79.

Louden, S H and Francis, L J (2003), *The Naked Parish Priest: what priests really think they're doing*, London, Continuum.

McCarley, N G and Carskadon, T G (1983), 'Test-retest reliabilities of scales and subscales of the Myers-Briggs Type Indicator and of criteria for clinical interpretive hypotheses involving them', *Research in Psychological Type*, 6, 24–36.

Macdaid, G P, McCaulley, M H and Kainz, R I (1986), *Myers-Briggs Type Indicator: atlas of type tables*, Gainesville, Florida, Centre for Application of Psychological Type Inc.

Mahon, D (1998), *Full Face to God: an introduction to the Enneagram*, London, Darton Longman and Todd.

Mitchell, W D (1991), 'A test of type theory using the TDI', *Journal of Psychological Type*, 22, 15–26.

Mowrer, O H (1960), 'Some constructive features of the concept of sin', *Journal of Counselling Psychology*, 7, 185–188.

Musson, D J (1998), 'The personality profile of male Anglican clergy in England: the 16PF', *Personality and Individual Differences*, 25, 689–698.

Musson, D J (2001), 'Male and female Anglican clergy: gender reversal on the 16PF5?', *Review of Religious Research*, 43, 175–183.

Musson, D J (2002), 'Personality of male Anglican clergy in England: revisited using the 16PF5', *Mental Health, Religion and Culture*, 5, 195–206.

Myers, I B (1998), *Introduction to Type: a guide to understanding your results on the Myers-Briggs Type Indicator* (fifth edition, European English version), Oxford, Oxford Psychologists Press.

Myers, I B and McCaulley, M H (1985), *Manual: a guide to the development and use of the Myers-Briggs Type Indicator*, Palo Alto, California, Consulting Psychologists Press.

Myers, I B, McCaulley, M H, Quenk, N L and Hammer, A L (1998), *Manual: a guide to the development and use of the Myers-Briggs Type Indicator*, Palo Alto, California, Consulting Psychologists Press.

Oswald, R M and Kroeger, O (1988), *Personality Type and Religious Leadership*, Washington, DC, The Alban Institute.

Palmer, H (1995), *The Enneagram in Love and Work*, New York, HarperSan-Francisco.

Pearson, P R (1983), 'Personality characteristics of cartoonists', *Personality and Individual Differences*, 4, 227–228.

Piedmont, R L (1999), 'Strategies for using the five-factor model of personality in religious research', *Journal of Psychology and Theology*, 27, 338–350.

Rawling, K (1992), *Preliminary Manual: the Cambridge Type Indicator: research edition*, Cambridge, Rawling Associates.

Reader, J (1996), Myers-Briggs: consciousness raising or a new narcissism?, in K Leech (ed.), *Myers-Briggs: some critical reflections*, pp. 31–34, Croydon, The Jubilee Group.

Rehak, M C (1998), 'Identifying the congregation's corporate personality', *Journal of Psychological Type*, 44, 39–44.

Reid, J (1999), 'The relationship among personality type, coping strategies, and burnout in elementary teachers', *Journal of Psychological Type*, 51, 22–33.

Richter, P and Francis, L J (1998), *Gone but not Forgotten: church leaving and returning*, London, Darton, Longman and Todd.

Robbins, M, Francis, L J, Haley, J M and Kay, W K (2001), 'The personality characteristics of Methodist ministers: feminine men and masculine women?', *Journal for the Scientific Study of Religion*, 40, 123–128.

Robbins, M, Francis, L J and Rutledge, C (1997), 'The personality characteristics of Anglican stipendiary parochial clergy in England: gender differences revisited', *Personality and Individual Differences*, 23, 199–204.

Rocklin, T and Revelle, W (1981), 'The measurement of extraversion: a comparison of the Eysenck Personality Inventory and the Eysenck Personality Questionnaire', *British Journal of Social Psychology*, 20, 279–284.

Ross, C F J (1993), 'Type patterns among active members of the Anglican church: comparisons with Catholics, Evangelicals and clergy', *Journal of Psychological Type*, 26, 28–35.

Ross, C F J (1995), 'Type patterns among Catholics: four Anglophone congregations compared with Protestants, Francophone Catholics and priests', *Journal of Psychological Type*, 33, 33–41.

Saggino, A and Kline, P (1995), 'Item factor analysis of the Italian version of the Myers-Briggs Type Indicator', *Personality and Individual Differences*, 19, 243–249.

Satava, D (1996), 'Personality types of CPAs: national vs local firms', *Journal of Psychological Type*, 36, 36–41.

Schurr, K T, Henriksen, L W, Moore, D E and Wittig, A F (1993), 'A comparison of teacher effectiveness and NTE Core Battery scores for SJ and a combined group of NJ, NP and SP first-year teachers', *Journal of Psychological Type*, 25, 25–30.

Sears, S J, Kennedy, J J and Kaye, G L (1997), 'Myers-Briggs personality profiles of prospective educators', *Journal of Educational Research*, 90, 195–202.

Siegman, A W (1963), 'A cross-cultural investigation of the relationship between introversion-extraversion, social attitudes and anti-social behaviour', *British Journal of Social and Clinical Psychology*, 2, 196–208.

Silberman, S L, Freeman, I and Lester, G R (1992), 'A longitudinal study of dental students' personality type preferences', *Journal of Dental Education*, 56, 384–388.

Stricker, L J and Ross, J (1963), 'Intercorrelations and reliability of the Myers-Briggs Type Indicator Scales', *Psychological Reports*, 12, 287–293.

Stricker, L J and Ross, J (1964), 'An assessment of some structural properties of the Jungian personality typology', *Journal of Abnormal and Social Psychology*, 68, 62–71.

Towler, R and Coxon, A P M (1979), *The Fate of the Anglican Clergy*, London, Macmillan.

Tsuzuki, Y and Matsui, T (1997), 'Test-retest reliabilities of a Japanese translation of the Myers-Briggs Type Indicator', *Psychological Reports*, 81, 349–350.

Tzeng, O C S, Ware, R, Outcalt, D and Boyer, S L (1985), Assessment of the Myers-Briggs Type Inventory items, *Psychological Documents*, 15, 17–18.

Vine, I (1978), 'Facts and values in the psychology of religion', *Bulletin British Psychological Society*, 31, 414–417.

Ward, H (1996), Myers-Briggs and the concern with techniques, in K Leech (ed.), *Myers-Briggs: some critical reflections*, pp. 6–11, Croydon, The Jubilee Group.

Ware, R, Yokomoto, C and Morris, B B (1985), 'A preliminary study to assess validity of the Personal Style Inventory', *Psychological Reports*, 56, 903–910.

Woods, R (1996), Spirituality, Jung, and psychological types, in K Leech (ed.), *Myers-Briggs: some critical reflections*, pp. 11–18, Croydon, The Jubilee Group.

GLOSSARY AND BIOGRAPHY

attitudes toward the outside world the two ways in which people approach the world around them: judging and perceiving

auxiliary function the psychological function which is preferred and developed second to the dominant function, and which provides support and balance for the dominant function

Cattell, Raymond B (1905–1998) psychologist who developed the theory of the Sixteen Personality Factor (16PF) model

character a person's moral and mental qualities which, unlike personality, are subject to change and development

coefficient alpha a test to show the extent to which all parts of a test work together reliably

correlation a measure of the degree of relationship between two variables

dichotomous opposite

dominant function the psychological function which is most preferred, most developed and most differentiated

empirical based on objective, scientifically verifiable data

extraversion within psychological type theory, extraversion is one of the two orientations, characterised by orientation toward the outer world within the Eysenckian model of personality, extraversion is a continuous dimension concerned with levels of sociability/reservedness

Eysenck, Hans J (1916–1997) psychologist who developed the theory of personality models based on orthogonal higher-order personality dimensions. His early models proposed the two dimensions of extraversion and neuroticism. His later model added the third dimension of psychoticism

factor analysis a mathematical method for establishing patterns in statistical data

fake-good attempting to manipulate personality test results in order to present a positive (but false) impression

feeling one of the two judging functions, characterised by decision-making based on subjective, interpersonal values

Francis Psychological Type Scales a self-report questionnaire designed to measure psychological type preferences by Leslie J Francis (2004)

hermeneutics the interpretation of scripture

inferior function the fourth psychological function, which is least preferred, least developed, and least differentiated; this function is always opposite to the dominant function

internal consistency the extent to which all parts of a test work together reliably

introversion within psychological type theory, introversion is one of the two orientations, characterised by orientation toward the inner world within the Eysenckian model of personality, introversion is the term employed to describe a low scorer on the continuous dimension of extraversion

intuition one of the two perceiving functions, characterised by perception focused upon meanings, patterns, and relationships

item analysis a mathematical method for testing how well individual items contribute to a scale

judging one of the two attitudes toward the outside world, characterised by a preference for structure, order, and closure

judging functions the two ways in which people make decisions and judgements: thinking and feeling

Jung, Carl G (1875–1961) Swiss psychologist who developed the theory of psychological types

Keirsey Temperament Sorter (KTS) a self-report questionnaire designed to measure psychological type preferences by David Keirsey and Marilyn Bates (1978)

Myers-Briggs Type Indicator (MBTI) a self-report questionnaire designed to measure psychological type preferences by Isabel Briggs and Katherine Myers (see, for example, Myers, McCaulley, Quenk and Hammer, 1998)

neuroticism a continuous dimension within the Eysenckian model of personality, concerned with levels of neuroticism/stability

orientations the two ways in which people direct their psychological energy: extraversion and introversion

orthogonal independent, uncorrelated variables

perceiving one of the two attitudes toward the outside world, characterised by a preference for flexibility, adaptability, and spontaneity

perceiving functions the two ways in which people gather information: sensing and intuition

personality theories models which account for differences in individual's characteristic patterns of thought, emotion and behaviour

psychoticism a continuous dimension within the Eysenckian model of personality, concerned with levels of toughmindedness/tendermindedness

processes the psychological processes are the perceiving process (sensing/intuition) and the judging process (thinking/feeling)

reliability the extent to which a test is both consistent and dependable; see **internal consistency** and **test-retest reliability**

sensing One of the two perceiving functions, characterised by perception focused upon facts, realities, and details

Sixteen PF A model of personality developed by Raymond B Cattell which proposes sixteen lower-order personality traits

tertiary function the psychological function which is preferred and developed third to the dominant and auxiliary function; this function is always opposite to the auxiliary function

test-retest reliability the extent to which the results of a test are consistent and dependable over time

thinking one of the two judging functions, characterised by decision-making based on objective, rational principles

type classification of individuals into sets of discrete categories based on their personality characteristics

trait an enduring and stable personality characteristic

validity the extent to which a test measures what it claims to measure

INDEX OF NAMES

INDEX OF SUBJECTS